1989

The Limits of Theory

The Limits of Theory

Edited, with an Introduction, by

Thomas M. Kavanagh

Stanford University Press *1989*
Stanford, California

Stanford University Press
Stanford, California
© 1989 by the Board of Trustees of the
Leland Stanford Junior University
Printed in the United States of America

CIP data appear at the end of the book

For Charlotte and Matthew

Acknowledgments

The idea for this collection of essays grew out of a series of lectures I organized at the University of Colorado, Boulder, during 1985 and 1986. I am indebted to Dean Everly B. Fleischer and the Graduate School Committee on the Arts and Humanities for their support of that series. René Girard, Michel Serres, François Roustang, Josué Harari, and Roy Roussel were invited speakers during that period, and this collection grew from the excitement generated by their addresses.

The translation into English of those essays originally written in French was carried out thanks to the generous efforts of a number of young scholars and friends. I would especially like to thank Gwen Wells (Descombes), Kate Gingrass (Serres), and Jan Owen, Sally Pane, and Carla Behrens (Rosset).

My gratitude goes also to the many friends who offered their support and help during this project: Bill Wolsky, John Waller, Clint Cline, Herb Alpern, Les Brill, Jim Palmer, and Dan Yang at Boulder, as well as Ross Chambers and John D'Arms at the University of Michigan.

Most of the texts in this volume are either original essays or appear here in translation for the first time. Michel Serres's essay is part of his *Les Cinq Sens* (1985). This translation is published by permission of Alfred A. Knopf, Inc., who will publish that entire book in a different translation in the future. Vincent Descombes's piece was originally published in French under the title "Les Embarras du référent" in *MLN*, 101: 4 (1986) and is published here by permission of the Johns Hopkins University Press. Clément Rosset's text consists partially of extracts from his *Le Réel: Traité de l'idiotie* (1977); Editions de Minuit has granted me permission to publish this translation. François Roustang's essay was first published as "De la relecture" in *MLN*, 101: 4 (1986) and is published here in translation by permission of the Johns Hopkins University Press. The translation appears in slightly abbreviated form in Roustang's *Quadrille of Gender: Casanova's Memoirs* (1988). Josué Harari's text is a revised version of a part of the seventh chapter of his *Scenarios of the Imaginary: Theorizing the French Enlightenment*. Copyright © 1987 by Cornell University. It is used here by permission of the publisher, Cornell University Press.

T. M. K.

Contents

Contributors

VINCENT DESCOMBES is professor of French at the Johns Hopkins University. He is the author of *Le Platonisme* (1971), *L'Inconscient malgré lui* (1977), *Modern French Philosophy* (1980), *Grammaire d'objets en tous genres* (1983), and *Proust: Philosophe du roman* (1987).

RENÉ GIRARD is Andrew B. Hammond Professor of French at Stanford University. Among his books are *Deceit, Desire and the Novel* (1966, 1969), *Violence and the Sacred* (1977), *"To Double Business Bound": Essays in Literature, Mimesis and Anthropology* (1978), *Scapegoat* (1985), *Job: The Victim of His People* (1986), and *Things Hidden Since the Foundation of the World* (1987).

JOSUÉ HARARI is professor of French at the Johns Hopkins University. He is the author of *Textual Strategies: Perspectives in Post-Structuralist Criticism* (1979) and *Scenarios of the Imaginary* (1987).

THOMAS M. KAVANAGH is professor of French at the University of Michigan. He is the author of *The Vacant Mirror: A Study of Mimesis Through Diderot's Jacques le fataliste* (1973) and *Writing the Truth: Authority and Desire in Rousseau* (1987).

CLÉMENT ROSSET is professor of Philosophy at the University of Nice. Among his books are *Logique du pire* (1971), *L'Anti-nature* (1973), *Le Réel et son double* (1976), *Le Réel: Traité de l'idiotie* (1977), *L'Objet singulier* (1979), *La Force majeure* (1983), and *Le Philosophe et les sortilèges* (1985).

ROY ROUSSEL is professor of English at the State University of New York at Buffalo. He is the author of *Conrad's Metaphysics of Darkness* (1971) and *Conversations of the Sexes* (1986).

FRANÇOIS ROUSTANG is a practicing psychoanalyst in Paris and visiting professor of French at the Johns Hopkins University. Among his books are *Dire Mastery* (1982), *Psychoanalysis Never Lets Go* (1984), *Lacan de l'équivoque à l'impasse* (1986), and *The Quadrille of Gender: Casanova's Memoirs* (1988).

MICHEL SERRES is professor of the History of Sciences at the University of Paris and visiting professor at Stanford University. Among his books are *Le Système de Leibniz* (1968, 1982), *Hermès I–V* (1969, 1972, 1974, 1977, 1980), *Jouvences: Sur Jules Verne* (1974), *Auguste Comte: Leçon de philosophie positive* (1975), *Esthétiques: Sur Carpaccio* (1975), *Feux et signaux de brume: Zola* (1975), *La Naissance de la physique dans le texte de Lucrèce* (1977), *The Parasite* (1980), *Rome: Le livre des fondations* (1983), *Genèse* (1982), *Les Cinq Sens* (1985), *L'Hermaphrodite* (1987), and *Statues* (1987).

The Limits of Theory

Introduction

Thomas M. Kavanagh

A growing and often preponderant concern with the presuppositions of reading has distinguished the study of literature in North America and Europe over the past few decades. Many critics have devoted themselves to elaborating and defending various critical theories by which, they argue, all analyses of literary works must justify themselves if they are to claim coherence and validity. Only within the framework of an explicit and potentially universal theory of literature, the recent history of literary study seems to tell us, can critics defend their discourse as something other than an exercise in idiosyncratic impressionism.

The authors contributing to this volume share the conviction that there is a limit beyond which this drive to theorize becomes something quite different from what it presents itself as being. Beyond that limit a transformation takes place, with liabilities and dangers that must be recognized to be understood.

The word "limit" is used here in its mathematical sense. It designates a frontier beyond which a change occurs, a border beyond which one thing becomes another. The title *The Limits of Theory* must not, in other words, be read as taking a position *against* theory, or as summarily dismissing the role and importance of theory. Attractive as that option may be for certain critics, it is a polemicist's illusion. In fact, no consideration of literature or any other cultural artifact can take place outside an at least implicit theory that both sustains and shapes its critical discourse. Murray Krieger has put the impossibility of our being, in any consequential way, against theory quite well: "Our choice is not between having a theory or not having one; for have one (or two or three or more incompatible ones) we must. Our choice is rather between having an awareness of those theoretical issues which our criticism inevitably raises or going along without such an awareness."[1] Arguing in a similar fashion, W. J. T. Mitchell points out that to espouse a position against theory is to make an integral move *within* the discourse of theory: "The antitheoretical polemic is one of the characteristic genres of theoretical discourse . . . an inevitable dialectical moment within theoretical discourse, the moment when theory's constructive, positive tendency generates its own negation."[2]

The contemporary preoccupation with theory has had as one of its effects the displacing of interest away from what is specific to any individual work and to-

[1] Murray Krieger, *Theory of Criticism: A Tradition and Its Systems* (Baltimore, Md., 1976), p. 7.

[2] See his introduction to *Against Theory: Literary Studies and the New Pragmatism*, ed. W. J. T. Mitchell (Chicago, 1985), p. 2.

ward the presuppositions and systemic cogency of the theoretical constructs that allow us to carry out our analyses. According to this position, the elaboration of an adequate theory of literature must become the central preoccupation of all critical discourse aiming at a significance beyond that of the belle-lettristic curiosity shop.

Movements as different from one another as structuralism, sociocriticism, psychocriticism, reader response theory, hermeneutics, and the various post-structuralisms share a preference for critical strategies that restrict their attention to elements that simultaneously are deduced from and consolidate a particular theoretical construct that traces out in advance the available repertoire of critical gestures. The theorist's statements about a given work thus become valid only to the extent they can establish themselves as particularizing corollaries to a general theory of literature assumed to be capable of so situating and so evaluating all possible literary works. The individual work itself becomes, in this scheme of things, a partial and inchoate exemplum whose analysis allows theorists to practice the higher art of elaborating synthetic, totalizing, and all-encompassing visions of the systems through which they speak.

As the predominant movement within literary studies over the past few decades, this trend has already begun to have profound effects on the university curriculum. Although the weight of institutional inertia may still favor established departmental enclaves, there is little doubt that, in terms of what is most contemporary and most potent in literary studies, disciplines such as the study of English and other national literatures find themselves dismissed as inevitably partial glimpses of local idiosyncrasies when compared to the far broader concerns of the literary theorist. And because the methodologies and findings of a whole series of other disciplines—history, philosophy, psychology, sociology, economics (the French *sciences humaines*)—must be expressed in language, they, too, are enjoined to recognize the hegemony of the theorists as the agents who can best inform parochial practitioners of what these disciplines are actually about.

The question this book asks is not whether or not theory should be practiced, but how far and toward what our concern with theory will take us. The contemporary hegemony of theory has, of course, provoked reactions of skepticism and even hostility. A strong countercurrent to the enterprise of theory can be traced in works stretching as far back as its current fashion: Susan Sontag, *Against Interpretation* (1964); Iain McGilchrist, *Against Criticism* (1982); Steven Knapp and Walter Benn Michaels, *Against Theory* (1982); Laurence Lerner, *Reconstructing Literature* (1983); Patrick Parrindor, *The Failure of Theory* (1986); and Frederick Crews, *Skeptical Engagements* (1987). These are only a few examples of what is now a vast and sometimes sadly reactive antitheoretical polemic.

As exaggerated and ultimately utopian as any *refusal* of theory must be, the motivations behind such a position are not incomprehensible to anyone involved with the institution that has created it. Anyone teaching theory to students, who, even within the more traditional disciplines, have long realized that they would do well to learn more of this brave new science, knows how ambiguous the results of such an undertaking can be. All too often our excitement at introducing students to the iconoclastic insights of Michel Foucault, Jacques Derrida, or Paul de Man seems to result, come time to read final papers, in a series of lifeless pastiches proving little more than that the students have learned to "speak" Foucault, Derrida, or de Man much as they might a foreign language, and this at the cost of all but total alienation from their own voices. Instead of being invigorated and broadened by their encounter with new and provocative ways of approaching the literary work, students too often become predictable epigones who, though easily classifiable in terms of their allegiances, are writing at the antipodes of what we had hoped their familiarity with theory would produce. What we had introduced as a discourse of the radically Other seems to have produced only the most resolute sameness and orthodoxy.

How is it, we must ask ourselves, that the encounter with theory can have so paradoxical a result? If anything, the agenda of theory, especially in its more recent, post-structuralist variants, seems to promise a nearly total freedom. No longer is the literary work seen as a repository of fixed meanings waiting to be identified and explicated by the properly assiduous reader. A teeming mass of free-floating signifiers that would be disfigured by any calcification into a single meaning, the liberated text becomes the site not only of freedom, but of an exhilaratingly candid opportunism. Richard Machin and Christopher Norris, in their recent introduction to a collection of critical essays entitled *Post-Structuralist Readings of English Poetry*, point out that "these readers favour a sort of interpretative opportunism: the importance of the text lies primarily in the way that it is made to enter current theoretical debate."[3] The old shibboleths of *coherence, unity, meaning,* and *intention*—all those terms signaling a reluctance on the work's part to do whatever the theorist might wish it to do—are cast aside in favor of a lucid recognition of what de Man has called "the autonomous potential of language"[4] and has equated with literariness itself. Literary theory, the work of an enfranchised and even opportunistic critic, is called upon to recognize itself as a creative activity in no way secondary to that of the literary work itself.

The individual work, like a once imprisoned and imprisoning spirit now set free by the force of theoretical insight, offers itself to the theorist as a promise of pure opportunity. Within the dynamics of this promised liberation, however, there occurs a methodological sleight of hand that must be identified and made explicit if we are to understand how it carries the enterprise of theory over the limit beyond which it becomes something else. The nature of this sleight of hand can be glimpsed in various definitions we

[3] Richard Machin and Christopher Norris, eds., *Post-Structuralist Readings of English Poetry* (London, 1987), p. 8.

[4] Paul de Man, *The Resistance to Theory* (Minneapolis, Minn., 1986), p. 10.

have recently been offered for the word "theory" it-self. Krieger, for instance, defines "theory" as "the systematic construct that accounts for and makes consistent the individual critiques of works of liter-ature" (p. 3). For Wlad Godzich, theory is "a system of concepts that aims to give a global explanation to an area of knowledge."[5] The use within these definitions of terms like "system," "consistent," and "global" to describe the theorist's work points to a startling dis-placement. All those characteristics of consistency and totality traditionally attributed to the literary work and the authorial intention presumed to moti-vate it are shorn from the primary text, only to reap-pear as the indispensable traits of any adequate the-oretical discourse.

The current usage of the word "text" is an impor-tant clue to what is happening here. "Text," it would seem, is what the work becomes when the locus of re-sponsibility for coherence and meaning is no longer situated in the work itself, but has been shifted to the theory speaking about the work. Machin and Norris again put it nicely: "Another characteristic of post-structuralist readings is their tendency to feature the text as an active speaker. Where once the author was, now shall the text be" (p. 3). Although their Freudian reference is certainly appropriate, there can be little doubt that, for writers like Machin and Norris, the word "text" is in fact little more than a discreet syn-onym for "theorist."

The decisive and determining role we might once

5 See Wlad Godzich's introduction to de Man's *The Resistance to The-ory*, p. xiii.

mistakenly have attributed to the author as master of
the work's intentionality has now become the exclusive prerogative of the theorist. It is the theorist's task
to give voice to an otherwise mute "text" that, without him, would remain forever cut off from its mul-
tiplicities of meaning and coherence.

The real risk of theory's moving beyond an intrinsic limit has, however, less to do with the potential
idiosyncrasy of such an understanding of its function
than with the intersubjective and political role theory
assumes when it is practiced within the institutional
context of the university. Godzich points to the necessarily intersubjective and political dimension of
theory when, in his introduction to de Man's *The Resistance to Theory*, he calls attention to the fact that
the meaning of the word "theory" is itself etymolog-
ically rooted in its diacritical opposition not, as we
might think, to *praxis*—to a program of practical
measures taken toward a defined goal—but to *aesthēsis* understood as a resolutely subjective aspect of
perception. Theory is the definitional opposite of *aesthēsis* (or feeling) because it is characterized by a compelling, "jubilatory" sentiment forcing its expression
beyond the sphere of individual, subjective perception and into the public realm. The word "theory,"
Godzich continues, derives from the Greek *theōrein*
(to see, to behold), but it refers to a particular kind of
seeing or beholding. Persons bearing the title *theōros*
in ancient Greece collectively constituted a *theōria*
only when they exercised their officially appointed
function of beholding and attesting to the occurrence
of an event. The establishment of the *theōria* as the

source of officially recognized testimony about what actually took place was seen as the only alternative to an otherwise infinite battle of individual claims and counterclaims, each marked by its own version of *aesthēsis*. From the first use of *theōria* by the Greeks, in other words, its function was the eminently political one of ensuring, says Godzich, that "between the event and its entry into public discourse, there is a mediating instance invested with undeniable authority by the polity" (p. xv). The role of theory was, from its inception, intimately linked to the institutionalized *power* of a group of authoritative viewers who might designate their vision as that which is officially sanctioned.

Making a similar point, the de Man essay Godzich introduces argues that the academy's discomfort with literary theory is first and foremost a discomfort with the power of language as language. With the assertion of such power, de Man claims, there inevitably arises "a resistance to the use of language about language. . . . to language itself or to the possibility that language contains factors or functions that cannot be reduced to intuition" (pp. 12–13). Intuition, for de Man—the assumption that language speaks immediately of the reality it reflects—inevitably blinds us to an understanding of language's properly rhetorical function. Theory, for de Man, is what becomes possible once language is recognized as having something other than, something more important than, a necessary and unproblematic referential function. The function of language in the literary work must not, he cautions us, be seen as an unproblematic mimesis of perception, consciousness, and experience opening directly on to such fundamentally non-theorizable questions as "considerations of truth and falsehood, good and evil, beauty and ugliness, or pleasure and pain" (p. 10).

In terms of its semantic history, then, the word *theory* has, curiously, moved from a function of authenticating what its very enunciation establishes as having actually taken place, as constituting public reality, to the quite different function of recognizing language's freedom in relation to any referent it might mistakenly be assumed to represent.

De Man's banishing of language's mimetic function within the literary text posits theory as a discourse cut off from all possible authentication by a meaning situated within the work independently of the theorist's discourse. Freed from any referential function, theory thus becomes the site of an unfettered *performance*, a performance in no way limited by any preexistent script. What we as readers of theory are called upon to behold is the ultimately self-grounding and self-justifying performance of the critic as theorist. A given theoretical reading establishes itself as valid and cogent not through any necessary adequacy or appropriateness to the inchoate text about which it speaks, but as a function of the skill and power with which the theorist's own linguistic performance convinces its audience of its value.

In the same way that meaning and coherence can no longer be said to characterize the literary work under discussion but only the theory elucidating it, so the only performance we as readers are called upon to appreciate is that of the theorist proposing his particular representation of the work. This establishment of theory as performance makes of it a discourse whose value must be judged not in terms of its congruence to the work under discussion, but in terms of its ability to compel assent from its readers. A valid theory becomes, more than anything else, one capable of eliciting the assent and adherence of its readers. Redefined in this way, the discourse of theory initiates, on an intersubjective level between theorist and reader, a dialectical and mutually sustaining redefinition of each by the other.

Any adequate understanding of this redefined relation between theorist and reader, between theory and audience, must begin by recognizing the fact that literary theory is first and foremost a creation of the modern university and its institutional ancillaries. As a dominant discourse, the production of literary theory is motivated by and functions within the specific practices and politics of the university as an institution devoted to teaching and publication. John Bayley has underlined the often obfuscated relation between university teaching and the rise of theory as follows:

Literary theory has never really come clean about its origins in the problem of teaching. As a substitute for knowledge it can appear highly effective, working as it does on the premise that knowing things is obsolete. There was far too much *stuff* there. Replace the great mass of it, which used to weigh on the memories and desires of youth, with a streamlined apparatus, crafted by professionals, and excitingly accessible to students once they have mastered the magic formulae.[6]

The formulae are magic, of course, in their power to open for the student the door to a university teaching position in which the student-become-mentor will then practice the same magic.

This notion of theory as a performance validated by its control of the audience and carried out within the context of the university helps us to discern more clearly the precise nature of the limit point beyond which theory becomes something else. By the nature of their relationship, theorist and reader, teacher and student are, respectively, a performer dependent on the reactions of his audience and an apprentice ultimately credentialed by his mentor. As such, they are always threatened by a potential *excess* within the dynamics of their relationship—an excess redefining the theorist as *master* and the student as *disciple*.

No context, from this point of view, is more prone to such a passage beyond the limit than the university as an institution. It is within our classrooms, and through the alliances and hostilities defining our profession, that the filiations of mutually sustaining masters and disciples function as a system defined by its own self-regulating structure of rewards and sanctions. It is clearly a question here of a politics, a politics demanding the brutal disqualification of all who would remain outside or speak against the mutually sustaining dialogues of masters and disciples. At the

6 John Bayley, "The Lost Instructors," *Times Literary Supplement*, Feb. 12–18, 1988, p. 167.

same time, when we examine the dynamics of any single master-disciple filiation, we discover that we are dealing with a joyfully oedipal politics—a politics of fathers and sons in which, paradoxically, the greatest rewards go not to the son who would slay the established father, but to the one whose self-approval remains forever grounded in the continuing approval of that elected father.

Although a given master and his disciples may form a self-sustaining and monolithic community or *school*, the scope of contemporary debate around theory precludes there being only one masterly voice. Even by the mid-1970's, the original structuralist dream of a potentially unified and universal *science of literature* was clearly an unattainable goal. If there is any one trait characterizing what is today loosely called post-structuralism, it is the explicit rejection of all theories pretending to universality. Instead we find a radical self-problematizing of language, which is recognized as an always self-sustaining and potentially other-deceiving array of rhetorical strategies. Because the texture of language reflects back on itself in an infinite loop, it becomes impossible in principle to exhaust the bristling rhetoricity of either the work under analysis or what any particular theory may already have said about that work.

Always dispersed, always a melee of different and differing cohorts of masters and disciples, literary theory within the university is, as it always has been, in a state of intense debate and rivalry. As with all such rivalry, the rivalry among theories leads to an in-

tensification of conflict, according to which rivalry
risks becoming its own obsessive object. In so doing,
in pushing theory beyond the limit, rivalry subverts
the project of theory by jeopardizing the possibility of
any real contact with the object over which the conflict rages.

Machin and Norris testify eloquently to the paradoxical consequences of this rivalry beyond the limit
in their introduction to what they describe as a series
of valiantly "incoherent" post-structuralist readings
of English poetry:

These essays are clearly far from irrational. Indeed, the very
rigour with which they are conducted, collectively and in-
dividually, is perhaps their most unsettling characteristic.
Each reading develops an insistent coherence of its own
that drives toward conclusive and irrefutable assertions.
But it does this while holding open the possibility of a multiplicity of competing meanings, each of which denies the
primacy of the others. (p. 7)

Anyone reading this claim cannot help but be in-
trigued by its effort to reconcile what is clearly irrec-
oncilable. The debonair ecumenism of "holding open
the possibility of a multiplicity of competing meanings" must at some point logically conflict with the
proclaimed project of developing "an insistent coherence . . . that drives toward conclusive and irrefutable assertions." The paradox at work in this claim is
important because, in its generous tolerance for radically antithetical interpretations, it shows quite
clearly the pressing need within the ideology of post-
structuralism for the possibility of a difference with-

out conflict. This illusion of the irenic coexistence of
contraries is essential not so much as a gesture of An-
glo-Saxon liberalism but because, in conjuring away
the intense rivalry so obviously a part of the contemporary debate around theory, it simultaneously denies that "loss of the real" concomitant with all such
rivalry.

Motivated by a perhaps repressed but nonetheless
compelling obligation to refute the dangerous errors
of their rivals, master and disciple provide each other
with the reciprocal assurance that they are secure
within their particular symbolic system, that they
themselves have achieved a position impervious to
the manipulations and mystifications inherent in the
rhetorics they analyze.

The propensity of any given theory to pass beyond
the limit, to serve unchecked the potential pathology
of the master-disciple relationship, is thus unrelated
to its grasp of the real, of the objects that theory
claims to explain and elucidate. On the contrary, a
given theory becomes most adequate to its own con-
solidation and propagation when the resolutely arduous and paradoxical nature of its discourse serves
to prolong and extend the progressively more self-en-
closed and self-sustaining dialogue of master and disciple as an arcane science accessible only through dil-
igent apprenticeship. The real itself, that about which
the theory claims to speak, becomes at best irrelevant
to this master-disciple dialectic. If the real is rejected,
held resolutely outside the symbolic system sustaining a given theory, it is because that reality always
brings with it a recalcitrant and dangerously unpre-

dictable challenge to the fantasmatic adequacy of the theory claiming to represent it.

When I speak of the real to which theory, beyond a certain limit, becomes extraneous, I mean to say that theory's potential enclosure within its own justification all too easily closes it off from any sense of the real as a concatenation of chance and circumstance, of the aleatory and the unpredictable. The real that theory elides should not be understood as some primordial given, as a presence or referent offering itself to unproblematic representation. Far more than any presence, the real is first and foremost an absence— the absence, precisely, of the progressively more monolithic certainties toward which the dynamics of the master-disciple dialogue push its participants.

It is against the background of this potential divorce between theory and the real that we might better understand what we saw to be the often perplexing results of "teaching theory." Why is it that a greater familiarity with the most stimulating works of contemporary theory should so often serve to homogenize and deaden the work of our students? What theory cannot teach, what any capitalization of its potential for intimidation and illusory mastery can only obfuscate, is a recognition of the fact that, as readers and writers rather than as masters and disciples, we are always and solely responsible for the value and interest of what it is we have to say. No allegiance to a given theory, and no promise of correctness concomitant with subservience to a given master, can take the place of an ability to communicate the sense of loss and discovery we can always legitimately demand of any act of reading. With our allegiance to a theory, with our apprenticeship as disciple to a master, comes a concern for correctness and orthodoxy that dispels any sense of *play*, any desire to *play with* the text and our reactions to it until the unpredictable happens, until something is discovered, until something works for us.

Teaching students to read, think, and write well about literature involves teaching them to recognize, exploit, and share—no matter how recalcitrant the text, no matter how aggressively and self-assuredly it remains within its own ideology—that sense of possibility, chance, and indetermination at the heart of every act of reading. But when the master's voice, constituting its readers as disciples, leaves them only the choice between repetition and silence, its exercise of theory beyond the limit obliterates all concerns save those with compliance and domination.

· It is in terms of this recognition of the limits of theory that a number of today's most innovative and seminal thinkers have begun to ask how theory functions, how it might be saved, and how it can preserve within its own discourse and its own discursive effects the freedom of reading, the elusive presence of the real, and the challenge of a voice speaking outside the various rhetorics of mastery.

The essays collected in this volume reject any notion of a return to some mythic moment before theory, to an idolatry of the virginal, untheorized text. They ask instead that we redefine and continue our practice of theory fully cognizant of what it is, of how it has been subverted into something else, and of what precisely is the limit point separating these two options.

The first of these, Michel Serres's "Panoptic Theory," is a provocative meditation on the special sight of "theory": how it works, what it does, and to what needs it responds. In addressing these questions, Serres weaves together strands from such divergent registers as classical mythology, the history of science, and the epistemology of suspicion. Using the omniscopic Argus as the central emblem of his analysis, Serres shows how the panoptic drive and the sciences it generates, deprived of any real object, inscribe themselves under the names of politics, representation, and language. Unconcerned with the object, they offer as real only the endless tokens of their own weakness and suspicion.

Addressing a more specific philosophical question, Vincent Descombes's "Quandaries of the Referent" examines the all-but-ubiquitous claim that the referential function of language is an "illusion." Looking at figures as diverse as Hegel, Koyré, Kojève, Hyppolite, Blanchot, and Lacan, Descombes examines how the "semiological hypothesis" has generated ever more distorted notions of the sign—notions adopted so that their proponents might maintain their allegiance to a theoretical model vitiated from the start.

Continuing this reflection on the philosophical premises of theory, Clément Rosset's "Reality and the Untheorizable" centers on the specific question of the real. Immediately with us and upon us, never allowing the *distance* necessary to any adequate theory, the real adamantly resists its absorption within the doubles of representation. To recognize the real as "idiotic," as forever singular and individual, is to refuse philosophy's abiding desire to replace it with its own verbal constructs, its theories as some *more real reality* we might dominate and through which we dominate the real.

The next four essays examine the specific practices of reading, criticism, and theory. François Roustang's "On Reading Again" enunciates a series of modest *principles* he feels must govern every act of reading—principles respecting the inherent violence, horror, and laughter that are part of every successful reading. Roustang's choice of principles over theory is a refusal of all preconceived certainties cutting us off from the work's ultimate voyage through uncertainty and indetermination.

Roy Roussel's "The Gesture of Criticism" is a parallel, mutually questioning reading of Paul de Man's *The Resistance to Theory* and Roland Barthes's *A Lover's Discourse*. This juxtaposition of a key theoretical text with an attempt to accommodate theory to the specificity of the personal allows an incisive analysis of how, as literary critics claiming both the expressiveness of the absolutely personal and an absolute transcendence of the personal, our discourse attempts an impossible reconciliation of clearly *knowing*, yet at the same time enthusiastically *being*, our own madness.

Josué Harari's "Nostalgia and Critical Theory" uses the example of Claude Lévi-Strauss's *Tristes Tro-*

piques to examine the unconscious strategies govern-
ing the elaboration of theory. Theory, for Harari, may
begin within the real, but it is within the real as a locus of agonizing and unmastered contradiction. The
power of theory thus derives not from its grasp of the
real, but from its production of abstract models opening the antinomies of the real to effortless manipulation and control. Expelling the real, theory nonetheless expresses an abiding nostalgia for what has
been lost in its choice of totality and closure.

My own "Film Theory and the Two Imaginaries"
examines the dual relation to the imaginary involved
in any attempt at film theory. While the pleasure of
film *viewing* is rooted in a profoundly personal and
unconscious imaginary, the pleasure of film *theory* is
rooted in an imaginary identification not with the
films themselves, but with an authority sanctioning
the theorist's own symbolic discourse. Poised between these two imaginaries, the brief history of film
theory is a cogent illustration of how theory, beyond
a certain limit, becomes the opposite of itself.

René Girard's "Theory and Its Terrors" is an iconoclastic analysis of how literary theory has come to
occupy so paramount a place in the teaching of literature. Examining the rise and fall of various disciplines within the university curriculum as well as the
mimetic rivalry among them,[7] this essay invites us to
recognize how theory's drive to dominate the individ-

---

[7] See on this same subject Gerald Graff, *Professing Literature: An Institutional History* (Chicago, 1987), as well as Tobin Siebers, *The Ethics
of Criticism* (Ithaca, N.Y., 1988).

ual work continues a mimetic violence presiding over the production of theory itself.

Each of these essays addresses from a different perspective what is perhaps the most paradoxical aspect of theory's current hegemony within literary studies. Those of us whose commitment to theory was born in the upheaval of the early 1970's, in theory's invigorating challenge to the way we understood the basic shape of knowledge, chose it as a refusal of the scholastic and deadening certainties of conventional literary history, of a comfortably isolated philology, and of self-perpetuating notions of the canon. Theory's promise lay in its resolve to recognize and confront the most fundamental property of the literary text: its status as a self-sustaining act of language. By so concentrating our attention on language as language, rather than on language as the reflection of something else (history, psychology, authorial intention, and so on), we felt we were advancing our understanding of the basic stuff of meaning, the fundamental semiotic processes through which everything calling itself knowledge was produced.

Our choice of theory was also the choice of something more clear-headed and honest than the reigning approaches to the literary work. Theory's foregrounding of language and rhetoric had to bring with it a commensurately greater self-awareness concerning our own writing, a salutary problematizing of our own discursive strategies. Never, we were certain, could theory, like so many other practices that call themselves scientific, hide its own rhetorical nature.

The hallmark of theory had to be a self-reflexive skepticism candidly pointing to its moves even as it made them, carefully refusing its authority even as it spoke authoritatively.[8]

Given that genesis, it is puzzling that, not even twenty years later, when we survey the intellectual tenor of the academy, we find that those repressive monoliths of the past against which we chose theory have disappeared with hardly a whimper. At the same time, embarrassingly enough, the one truly healthy orthodoxy, secure in its authority and imperial in its practices, is that of literary theory and its various methodologies.

Confronted with so paradoxical a sea change, we can only conclude that what we lost sight of was precisely that limit, that boundary, that frontier beyond which the enterprise of theory, in terms of its original impetus, has become the opposite of itself. These essays are attempts to understand how that transformation has occurred, what price we pay by ignoring it, and how the practice of theory might once again fulfill its original promise.

[8] I am indebted here to Ross Chambers for sharing with me his different convictions on these questions.

The Problematic

Panoptic Theory

Michel Serres

L et us speak of the peacock, a bird twice monstrous, which wears so many feathers, and such long ones, that it cannot fly. As though evolution had made a mistake, by excess, it shows us a hundred eyes we dream can see, but know cannot. When it struts, it shows an ocellated tail on which it exposes only feather eyes. Let us speak of those eyes.

One day the peacock crossed Hermes' path, who was then called Argus, a man who could see every-thing. Argus had, they say, two pairs of eyes, one in front on his face like everyone, another in the back of his head. No dead angle. Others say he had a hundred eyes, fifty in front and as many on his neck. Still others say he had an infinite number of eyes strewn everywhere on his skin. Clairvoyant at the beginning of the tradition, he is a figure who becomes at the end of his fantasmatic growth pure eye, an ocular globe of eyes, a skin tattooed by eye-shapes. Growth and fantasy often accompany each other. Argus sees everywhere and is always watching. He sleeps with only one pair of eyes at a time or with only half his eyelids closed. Half asleep, half awake. The best of those watchers of the earth and the air, he deserves his nickname of Panoptes, the panopticon.

An excellent example of perfect vision and lucid skin, Panoptes would today have been highly prized for his penetrating view of the world and for his careful experiments. He would have held the first place in our laboratories, in our observatories, and even out in the field. He would have kept his watch marvelously. We must pay constant attention to things in our sciences and on our voyages.

In those times, however, in those mythic times, Argus was used for surveillance. Panoptes, employed by Hera, the jealous wife, becomes a spy of Zeus's marginal loves. He will be placed in the middle of the gods' marital relations, of Jupiter's affair with a nymph.

The observation of things or the surveillance of relations. There is a huge difference. Two worlds, perhaps, oppose themselves there. Two epochs: that of myth and that of our own history.

The attentive examination of objects does not interest myth; Argus will become a private detective. Blessed with a hundred eyes that are open while the other hundred rest, he is a policeman, a prison guard, a warder: a specialist in all kinds of shadowing.

Culture becomes refined when it displaces its look from relations among men to innocent objects. Our morale, that amiable suppleness of a lightened collective life, improves when our attention is diverted away from those uneasy loves clumsily experienced by our neighbors or from their political opinions and

toward the trajectory of a comet. A society dominated
by surveillance is aged, old, outdated, abusively archaic. Only the past lives there. Monstrous itself, it
shows every sign of the age of myth.

Surveillance and observation. The human sciences
are a surveillance; the exact sciences are an observation. The first are as old as our myths; the others, new,
were born with us, and are only as old as our history.
Myth, theater, representation, and politics do not
teach us how to observe; they commit us to a surveillance.

Panoptes sees everything, always and everywhere.
For which task do the gods employ him: for surveillance or for observation?

In its Greek meaning, the verb "to see" incarnates
theoretical man, an omnidirectional ball of open
eyes. What purpose does theory serve? The surveillance of relations, or the examination of objects?

I shall call poor that which has no object. Myth has
no object, nor does theater or politics.

We had few objects in the past, long ago, once upon
a time. This state of a humanity with few things has
not been erased from our memory. Poor in things, our
wealth then consisted of men. We spoke only of them
and of their relations. We lived in and on our relations.
I call myth poor, then, without objects. I call poor the
theater, deprived of things; theories are poor; politics
is poor. Our philosophies are poor and miserable. Our
human sciences are poor.

We remember so well that state of poverty that we

cannot help but recognize it when we come upon it, here and there, in the countries of the world, in our stories or in our abstract discourses. We have barely emerged from places, families, and collectivities that were deprived of things and where for so long we were thrown back only on our relations. Destitution encourages surveillance and informing. The villages of my childhood hummed with watchful and talkative Arguses. Everyone knew everything about everyone—as if, in our very midst, a panoptical tower watched over us like the token of some indiscreet social contract or inevitable police contract. No one paid attention to things, or very little. Everyone monitored the relations of everyone to everyone else. I have known societies composed entirely of sociologists. They had an incredible talent for watching and storytelling. We have only barely emerged from that antiquity; and not all of us have emerged from that poverty, which lasted from the age of myth until yesterday. I can remember mythic societies that were completely caught up in representation, completely asleep in language. Poverty is measured not only by bread but by words; not only by the lack of bread but by an excess of words, by an excess bordering on exclusivity, by a prison of words. Language expands when bread is lacking. When bread comes, our mouths, long starved, have too much to do also to occupy themselves with speaking. We have learned to love objects.

No object circulates on the floorboards of a theater. Spectacles and words are offered to those who have only words. Our theories are empty of objects; they

watch only our relations. Ask philosophy for bread, it
pays you back with good words and representations.
Ask it for bread, it has only circuses. It lives on relations, on the human sciences; it lives on myth and antiquity, never leaving the village of our childhood. It
has no world, it produces no things, it furnishes no
bread. For how long have we been able to call it poor,
poor and starved, as was our youth?

A prosperous and productive philosophy would
provide as much bread as anyone wanted to whom-
ever passed by.

The proliferation of objects, the exponential deluge
of things, has led us to forget the time of their absence.
And that time now seems to us so old! Archaic, an-
tediluvian—yes, mythic. Our myths and our philosophy tell us about that time. Memories of places
where lovers were watched in an empty and resonant
space, where no one ever thought of eating. Thus philosophies that lack objects (almost all of them), philosophies that derive their values only from the human sciences (almost all of them), are aged and poor.
They seem so old to us that we read them as we read
myths. One might think they were politics, or theater, or magic. Whenever, by chance, they come upon
an object, they change it, by the stroke of a magic
wand, into a relation, into language, into representation.

Philosophies pull us backward. All things considered, the observer is worth more than the watcher, the
detective or the policeman. The astronomer who falls

to the bottom of the well is worth more than the woman who, behind his back, scorns him to her friends. Who is truly present to the real—the man who stares at the stars, or the woman who hides behind him to comment on the ridiculous scene? Do the washerwomen know that a well makes an excellent telescope and that, from the bottom of its vertical cylinder, the only telescope known to antiquity, one can see the stars in broad daylight? What do they have to laugh about? They don't realize that the scientist has knowingly descended into the chasm. Those writers of fables who still make us laugh, do they realize it? And the philosophers? It is better to move from relations to things (a demanding itinerary) than to return to relations from objects (an easy practice). From science to theater, from work to politics, from descriptions to myth, from watching the star as a thing to its comical representation. The exact sciences were formed with the emergence of the object; they aided its emergence. To go backward is frightening: letting objects once again become relations, stakes, fetishes, commodities. Regressions. A bit of naïveté is a progress over suspicion.

Inundated by objects, we dream about relations as though they were some lost paradise. Their paradise was in fact a quite ordinary hell, peopled by voyeurs and willing policemen, oozing suspicion, while laziness battled politics for control. The philosophy of suspicion is the oldest profession in the world. Communities deprived of objects, either by their own wish or by the cruelty of others, give themselves over to the

delights of policing, of the political jail. They con-
demn themselves to the hell of relations. Inversely,
their masters do not want objects. This is proof that
things deliver us from surveillance, that observation
frees us from suspicion.

The sciences that have no objects know only the
methods of the detective or the policeman; they are a
part of myth. Objective knowledge makes up our present history; the human sciences, which are ancient,
take us back to mythology. Observation weaves in the
light of day what surveillance undoes in the dark of
the night. Of whom should we be afraid?

Hermes is going to kill Panoptes. The bearer of
messages will prevail over the watcher as he spies and
notes. Communication and information kill theory.
How?

Zeus, the king of the gods, loves Io, the beautiful
nymph. Hera, his queen, suffers from jealousy. The
jealous are condemned to live in that thorny place
where surveillance is born; a jalousie is a place from
which one watches. Zeus is unfaithful to Hera. And
he cheats: he transforms the nymph into a heifer.
Who, me, love an animal? She shines, nevertheless,
with her marvelous whiteness, her smooth hide.

Hera is suspicious. Hera has her doubts about the
bull who circles the cow. She too knows the trick and
can transform beings as easily as Zeus can. She sends
a gadfly, her own thorny envy, to sting the heifer and
to panic her, to force her to leave. Io, forlorn, gallops

to Europe, giving her name to the Ionian Sea as she runs along its beach, and flees into Asia by that place since called the Bosporus, the step of the cow. A vagabond, she suffers and complains, sad to be loved by a god, as unhappy in her wandering and in her love as was Prometheus, crucified in vengeance and immobility.

Hera has guessed correctly. Zeus was, in fact, hiding beneath the appearance of the bull.

The queen, frustrated, calls upon Argus, from whose sight nothing escapes. Panoptes spies on the cow, and even Zeus can do nothing about it. The king finds himself held in check. Theory, panoptical, jealously watches all from the height of its tower.

In the human sciences, dealing only with relations, it is the suspicion of the policeman or the inquisitor that determines the method. It is a method that spies, tracks, sounds hearts and loins. It asks questions and doubts the answers, but it never asks itself: By what right does it behave in this way?

God is not a trickster, they say in the exact sciences, where the innocent object remains loyal and trustworthy. God doesn't deceive; he stays within the rules of the game he has set up. But man does deceive in the human sciences, and worse, he cheats. In the exact sciences, since God does not deceive, there is no reason for him to cheat. In the human sciences, man deceives and cheats. Man is not only subtle, like the God of the exact sciences, not only complex and refined; he also hides his hand, trickily, pretending to have another strategy and then suddenly changing the rules, cheating, playing outside the rules of the game. Man cheats in the social sciences, where the abuse of the rules is law, where changing the rules is the only rule.

The exact sciences construct theories that are subtle yet loyal, refined and stable. A cat remains a cat: a principle of identity. The human and social sciences describe theories that are even more underhanded than fraud, more tricky than trickery, in order to foil their object. Here, everything becomes possible. A cow is a woman or a god is a bull—even the principle of identity varies. Reason watches while reason sleeps; reason sleeps as it watches in this hell of relations where even stability fluctuates.

Underhandedly or behind your back, the human sciences multiply the worst practices. The term "hypocrisy" describes this movement well. Always behind the object or the relation, their method is critical, hypocritical. It swindles the swindlers, deceives the deceivers, hides behind the cheaters' backs. It steals from the thieves, polices the policemen, teaches a trick or two to the most famous detectives, interrogates the Grand Inquisitor, spies on the travelers, betrays the liars, studies the weak and the poor, and exploits all of them as it collects its information: their little secrets, the last thing they have left.

The hypocritical method consists of always placing yourself behind the other, thus creating a line. You must jump quickly to the end of the line, get behind that last person who has necessarily left his own back exposed, and then cover your own back for fear of being caught by whoever has understood the stratagem. Whence the rules of the method: for the liar, an even bigger liar; for the pervert, an even greater pervert (a kind of plupervert, by analogy with the pluperfect); for the voyeur, the theoretician.

The movement has no limit. It constructs extended chains of reasons, monotonous and difficult, which try to close in on themselves. In other words, philosophies that base their theories on the human sciences try to occupy sites that will themselves escape all criticism; they try to find the outer limit of the chain or the end of the line. They are addicted to reasoning by *extrema*, just as, during the classical period, the philosophies that based themselves on the nascent exact sciences tried to reach the divine limit point, the site of that never-deceiving god of the philosophers and the scientists. God can neither deceive himself nor deceive us—there is the limit point. Here, in the case of the human sciences, the limit point would be at the opposite extreme: to cheat or to deceive so totally that all imaginable cheating will always already be expected and accounted for. The panopticon, extra-lucid and inescapable, has always already seen everything.

Has our traditional theology of knowledge and evil foreseen these closures at the limit points? They would be the Devil and God.

To the God of those philosophers and scientists who dominated the classical period and the emergence of modern science, does our own age of the social sciences oppose the Devil as a new maximal site?

God does not deceive or cheat. Objects, in the exact
sciences, remain stable. Man does deceive and cheat,
so much so that he sometimes disappears, as did Zeus
under the bull's skin or Hera under the gadfly's
stinger.

He who cheats and deceives does so because he
wishes to win. Therefore, the first of God's attributes
consists of caring nothing about winning.

Detach yourself from the stakes, forget about vic-
tories and losses, and you will enter the realm of science, observation, discovery, thought.

Here one might define exactly two maximal sites:
an apex of stability and confidence, and an extremity
of distrust. To the stability of objects there corresponds the instability of relations.

Since the classical period, God watches over the exact sciences. Some say he guides them; others say he
favors them. The Devil watches over the human sciences, the ultimate limit of deceit and trickery. He
uses extreme and exquisite ruses to defeat the power
and the goodness of God, to take or retake God's place.
God deploys no ruses, he abandons all struggle. The
war between the Devil and God has never taken place.
The one wants to win, the other wants nothing.

Indifferent to winning and to losing, outside the
arena of victory and defeat, beyond all systems of
measurement, God is infinite. And thus we might define the infinite as an indifference to the battle of all
the devils.

Free from the hell of relations, God devotes himself
to the object; therefore, he creates the world, the in-

tegral of all obejcts. Everything, therefore, flows from his leaving the game.

Hera and Zeus play chess to trick each other or to win, devil against devil, the worst cheaters. The Devil is the god of myths, or of our human sciences. Our thought is shaped by his regressive reign.

Could we conceive of a new man who would pay no heed to cheating or deceiving, freed from the obligation to mount the winner's podium where victory is the only prize?

Panoptes, positioned at one extreme, sees everything, knows everything; nothing escapes him. The myth, with its falsely naïve images, easily describes concepts that we can formulate only with difficulty. In a game, the point is to discover unbeatable moves. Whence the construction of extremes: God, the Devil, Panoptes himself, Hera the queen, and Zeus the king. The strongest defy the strongest, as during the rutting of deer.

Zeus wants to deceive his wife, who wants to catch him. Zeus cheats: there, where you see a cow, a woman passes. Hera cheats: the gadfly takes off and stings according to her will. The goddess Hera places herself behind the god Zeus, who places himself behind her. Zeus hides his tricks from her who hides her own from him. An indefinite game. Each of them has a back and thus offers a weak spot and blind opening to the other.

Let us seek, therefore, a third man, who cannot be gotten around. Let us imagine someone who has no back: insomniac, with no dead angle, no blind spot,

without lapses or unconsciousness, intensely present, an integral of faces, an omnidirectional ball of
eyes, a geometric form made up of living facets watching and sleeping in bursts and fade-outs, like a lighthouse on the coast—or, even better, like an ensemble
of fires and signals reigning over an area and populat-
ing the night—who looks and calls, blinking uncer-
tainly: Argus. Here, at last, is the total theory, the unbeatable method that will vanquish all. You cannot
slip past Argus's body. Here, at last, is the perfect position for those who want the first or last place. This
is the position for those who would critique while
never being critiqued: an observing presence with no
observable opacity; always a subject, never an object.
No one can take Panoptes from behind, he has no behind, no underneath. He is an all-scrutinizing sphere.

Those who concern themselves with men and who
therefore reign over them always establish themselves in a dead angle, on the dark, blind, and powerless side of the active and present subject, behind his
back. Sickness offers an opening, as does sleepiness,
misery, the poverty of language, the residual unknown of collective relations, or childish hope. The
doctors of bodies or of souls, the economists, the politicians, the rhetoricians live in this dead angle. They
stand in the blind spot, themselves sheltered from all
blindness, in the dark of the unconscious or in the
trembling of tears. They see without being seen, each
finding his own unsilvered mirror or his jalousie. The
philosopher who summarizes and typifies them, who
integrates and reflects them, becomes panoptical. He
is inescapable, unbeatable, like Argus.

You who watch everything with always open eyes, is your lucidity never bathed in tears?

Here is the state of the game in progress: Zeus himself check and mate. The queen beats the king with her panoptic rook. Zeus calls upon his knight. Hermes passes. The king puts him to good use; he orders him to kill Panoptes.

It is impossible to approach or to surprise Panoptes. There is no surprise for the man committed to surveillance. (Notice the prefix *sur*, which marks this strategy of the more, the always more.) The knight must slip past the rook no one can slip past. How?

Hermes puts Panoptes to sleep. He plunges him into a magical sleep by playing the syrinx as others might charm serpents with their flutes. Hermes invents the syrinx, or panpipes, for this battle.

A new battle has developed between extremes. Panoptes possesses the integral of sight. He offers no opening to any adversary as far as sight is concerned. Hermes thus leaves that terrain, on which Argus is unbeatable, and moves to the realm of sound, employing its integral: whence the name of the panpipes—Pan against Panoptes. (Notice the prefix *pan*, which marks this strategy of total war.) Hearing against sight, a strange conflict of faculties. Ear against eye, integral opposed to integral, panoply against panoply, the sum of waves balancing the sum of evidence. An ichnography of intuitions against a geometry of messages, a fabulous struggle in an inconceivable space, the system of harmony envelops the theory of representation.

Suddenly, this fantastic battle between giants and gods, all-powerful against all-powerful, Devil and God, Jupiter and Juno, Pan and Panoptes, is reduced to a seemingly simple confrontation. The syrinx puts Argus to sleep; the cobra twists unthreateningly, listening to the sound of the Indian flute. Where does this fascinating magic come from? The enchantment comes from song. What power does the ear have over the eye, sound over sight, listening over looking?

A visible event is localized, it can be situated in terms of distance and angle, it shares coordinates with all the visible events around it. We occupy a point of view; we perceive profiles; our sight defines a place. The panoptical myth would force this place, furiously multiply its definitions. Just as Leibniz summed up the scenographies of a given thing in order to obtain its ichnography or its geometral, so Panoptes integrates all points of view in his body, sums up all the sites from which he sees. God alone, for Leibniz, can behold all the profiles of a given thing in a single moment. Argus alone, the rounded ball, presents himself as an eye made up of eyes—a faceted vision like that of the fly. A real asset, but a feeble one, or rather a limited one, because even the best watcher, as a geometric subject, sees the spatial sum of the things around him, but sees each thing only as a profile, which is quite different from being able to see it as a geometric object. His body, limited to one place, is like a lighthouse, round like its lantern, diffusing pencils of light in all directions, receiving the flash of objects at all points on its sphere.

A sound has no specific place; it occupies space. If

its source is often vague, its reception is broad and generalized. Sight betrays a presence; sound does not. Sight distances, music touches, noise besieges. Absent, ubiquitous, omnipresent, rumor envelops bodies. The enemy may intercept a radio transmission, but he cannot block our transmitter: sight remains discrete, sound waves escape us. Our sight leaves us free, our hearing encloses us. The same person who can escape a scene by lowering his eyelids or covering his eyes with his fists, or by turning his back and running away, cannot escape a clamor. No wall, no ball of wax is enough to stop it. All matter vibrates and conducts sound, especially flesh. A black veil blinds, is hermetically closed to light, and other bodies may obstruct other passages; but Hermes knows a vehicle that itself knows no hermetic walls. Sight is local; hearing is global. Far more than the ichnography, which is geometric for the subject or the object, hearing is marked by ubiquity, by an almost divine power to capture the universal. The optical is singular; the acoustical is total. Hermes the passe-partout transforms himself into a musician because sound knows no obstacle: the beginning of the total ascendancy of the verb.

We are speaking here simultaneously of magic, of philosophy, of common sense and of the world as it is. Pan bewitches Panoptes by overwhelming his sound-conducting flesh. The strident sound makes his eye-strewn skin vibrate, his muscles tremble, his tears flow, his skeleton shake. The clairvoyant ball is overwhelmed by a lake of tears; Argus collapses with emotion. The global vanquishes the sum of strategic sites. The integral, vainly sought by an adding up of sites or points of view, by a juxtaposition of eyes, is effortlessly and immediately overwhelmed by the wave. Have you ever encountered a work that effortlessly succeeded, on the first attempt, at what a hundred thousand other works, spread out over a lifetime, never managed to accomplish? Did you not cry? Argus crumbles. As panoptical and lucid as this clear sphere may be, it remains differential and pointillist, an analysis of tiny states or dwarfed scenes. As awkwardly as a sound may begin, it immediately manages to impose itself on its surroundings. Its victory is magical, if you wish, but it is one wrought by the senses. Sound vanquishes sight, or fascinates it. Sight fixes itself on the extreme limit of a narrow beam, and that beam becomes our vision. Sound puts sight back in its place.

Thus Leibniz, in his infinite quest of the unintegrateable sum of all ichnographies, completed his system with the notion of a Universal Harmony. Representation, even panoptical representation, falls asleep when Harmony resounds. Better still, if we are able to formulate the idea of a world or of God, or even of a system, if we are able to arrive at totalities, we are never in fact led to them by partial or interminable representations but only by harmony, by the music of a metaphysical Pan.

By marginal magic, ordinary sense, or high philosophy, we obtain the same result: Pan defeats Panoptes. The myth sets forth in simple acts, perfectly summed up or integrated, what we only disperse in our discourses and disciplines. But the world, everywhere around us, shouts out this same result. By this I mean the environment that we have prepared or constructed, and that plunges us into an inextinguishable din. For how long now have we been asleep, drugged by noise and music, unable to see, unable to think? Hermes has taken power over the entire world. Our technological world exists only as an integral of the tohubohu. You can no longer find anything on earth— not the ground, not a furrow, not a small insect, not the slightest hollow—that is not covered by the diluvian waters of our racket. The great Pan has won, he has chased all silence from space. If you would have pity on me, show me where to think.

The panpipe pierces and disturbs. One June evening I was waiting for a total eclipse of the sun, standing on a terrace facing a yard, in front of a maple tree, during those bygone years when the days ended in silence. It soon grew dark. The eclipse, like a wave, was passing over when suddenly there erupted at my neighbor's a kind of savage dance punctuated by the piercing, astringent, strange sounds of the panpipe. Some young people were celebrating some occasion. They had confused the eclipse's shadow with twilight and were celebrating the entry into night. For all our knowledge, the veiling of the sun's light troubles to the point of discomfort and carries us into another world. Pan led me there; I knew he had blinded the sun and my sight, swept space under the wave of wind, covered normal appearances with an orange, purple, and teeth-gnashing green hue. Horrified, I listened for the arrival of some sort of cruel and complicated Aztec gods.

Here is the second phase of the game: Hera herself is check and mate. The king takes the queen's rook by moving his knight. Nothing more is said of Io, crying, wandering toward the Caucasus Mountains, near the chained Prometheus, a virgin at the foot of the cross; nothing more is said of her except by those who weep for the sorrows of the world. Hermes has put Panoptes to sleep and killed him; everyone is talking about the murder.

Argus's site is only local, no matter how far his vision might extend. He integrates all the information available from a given point, without fault or mistake; he is a refined analyst. Hermes intercepts all information in all places, transfers and translations, interferences and distributions. He occupies the passageways. Argus holds one tactical position; Hermes has taken the strategic sites. The first will win the battle; the other will win the war. Argus, intensely present, detects all presences; but Hermes, who is everywhere, need not worry about presence; he can be absent in his ubiquity. The police block all the roads, they are no longer concerned with following. They no longer need any watcher, here and now. Everything changes when presence is no longer the only beginning.

From light, Panoptes has taken its clarity; Hermes

has taken its swiftness of the arrow. Until recently, classical philosophy placed itself under the sign of illumination. Contemporary philosophy is discovering the speed of lightning. The speed of light wins out over its purity. Consider the novelty of this victory: the principal quality of a theory or of an idea—its most traditional value, clarity—finds itself overtaken by the speed of its passage. Pan or Hermes kills Panoptes: the speed of the message is worth more than the lucidity of the thought. We are speaking about the new state of knowledge.

We are speaking about common sense and about philosophy. At the same time, we are describing our world. Our network of communications renders presence useless, the network has no center, it makes surveillance obsolete. Audio-visual or computerized circuits make the guard towers of the last war, borrowed from Roman camps, seem laughable. Sailors navigate without watching for lighthouses, their protection guaranteed by listening devices and tracking screens. Whoever can control as he wishes our codes and their circulation in space can let his watchers rest: they may fall asleep on their watches listening to music. The murmuring passage of messages puts the watchdog, the spy, and the informer to sleep; it anesthetizes the warder. With space better controlled, with prisons more tightly secured, with our telephones, televisions, and telecommunications, all the avatars of Panoptes are sent on vacation, and with them all those figures for whom presence remains present—yes, all those successive figures of phenomenology.

Hermes the spirit, everywhere present, suddenly descends into space.

Hermes the network replaces all the local posts, all the watchtowers juxtaposed in space or as successive figures in time: his geometral disqualifies all phenomenology.

We are speaking at the same time of common sense, of listening and hearing, and soon of the word and of the code; of music and of song; of drugs and of anesthesia, by a forgetting of presence or by a loss of intuition. We are speaking of newspapers, of magazines, of police or politics—the struggle of Pan against Panoptes takes place there every day; we are speaking of a new state of knowledge. We are speaking of relations and of objects, of knowledge and of surveillance, of competition and of society. The informational world takes the place of the observed world; things known because they are seen cede their place to an exchange of codes. Everything changes, everything flows from harmony's victory over surveillance. Gnoseology changes, as does epistemology, but so does daily life, the changing niche into which our bodies are plunged, and so does behavior, and therefore ethics and education.

Only a short time ago we clung, with our notions of observation, clarity, and intuition, to things themselves as though they were moorings, ties, or anchors. Theory, by its own admission, existed under the sign of sight and of a phenomenology of appearances given over to optics. Those moorings now give way. The message becomes the object itself. The code states the given, the data bank has taken the place of the world.

Or rather: the message once again becomes the given, as it did in the course of what I have called antiquity, when the collectivity nourished itself on its relations and its messages, out of a contempt for or forgetfulness of objects. Relations return, bringing with them the heavy and regressive burden of stakes and fetishes, the whole of mythology. Science, ahead, races toward its premises. Wealth leads back to poverty. Increased productivity reproduces a state of poverty. Pan kills Panoptes: the age of the message kills the age of theory. Will the human sciences reabsorb the exact sciences as they did in antiquity? As they tell us of it in myth?

War will be declared in the sciences, an always more devastating war. We will see its secrets and its ruses reflower. Jealousy will reach even to the skies, where the gods, old lovers decayed with age, still dedicate themselves to their struggle unto death.

Multiplied by rigor and efficiency, will the hell of relations return?

Tired of these deceitful games, of these tricks, dreaming that our brief lives might escape this monotonous cycle of blood and death, we hope to return to a moment of trust that neither deceives nor cheats; we hope for a theory of knowledge that reunites the exact and human sciences. A new knowledge, a new epistemology, a new man, a new education: we will escape our collective death only on that condition.

Meanwhile, Hera, check and mate, plays on. She strips dead Argus, she takes from the watcher his pan-optical skin—a floating tatter spotted with its closed eyelids—and drapes it over the plumage of her favor-ite bird, the peacock. Of the omnidirectional ball of intense eyes there remains only the double color of the eyes and their shimmering pattern, a fascinating and silky fan. The immobile fowl, crying raucously and out of tune as Hermes plays the pipes, bending low as Hermes passes in flight, will show us, should it proudly strut, our dead theory. Sight looks blankly upon a world from which information has already fled. A disappearing species, only ornamental, the peacock asks us to admire, in the public parks and gar-dens where gawkers gather, the old theory of repre-sentation.

Philosophical Premises

The Quandaries of the Referent

Vincent Descombes

The following should be read as an outline for a historical and logical note on the notion of the referent.

Critics and philosophers are often called upon to take a stance on what might be called the "referential function of language." They must, for instance, decide whether in reading a text we refer back to *referents* (or to *the referent*) outside the text, whether we refer to other texts, or whether we must instead remain within the text we are reading.

I intend to show that such discussions need not be taken seriously. Does language turn outward toward something else, or inward toward itself? Does a book refer to the world, or only to *a* world constructed in the book? To find any single answer to these questions would be quite surprising. It is far more interesting to try to understand why we feel a need to speak of the referent, and what help we can expect from this concept.

The Linguistic Turn

At the end of the last century, the focus of discussion was not the referent, but the *object*: the object of representation. The question posed was that of the limits of our representational capacity, and the urgency of the question came from the priority then given by philosophers to the epistemological question: How can I know something? If our ability to represent things is limited, so also will be our ability to know them. Hence the question in relation to any given thing: How can this thing become the object of my representation?

The epistemological question thus mandated a return to the examination of the mental faculties of the subject engaged in representational activity. But this meant entrusting the foundation of all knowledge to a single discipline that was, moreover, naturalistic. This in turn gave rise to the objection of psychologism. Another way of approaching the problem had to be found. Philosophers, for their part, defined that other way of examining the limits of representation a *transcendental* examination. Such a philosophical path was, obviously, speculative and unsatisfactory to those "researchers" who sought a positive or quasi-scientific solution to the problem. It was at this point that there occurred what has been called "the linguistic turn in philosophy"[1] and the rise of linguistic theory.

[1] Richard Rorty, *The Linguistic Turn: Recent Essays in Philosophical Method* (Chicago, 1967).

If we were to take this linguistic turn seriously, we would assign the following significance to the exchange of the new *referent* for the old *object*. So long as there was talk of the object, we would say, it was imagined that human beings had direct access to things. The mind looked out onto things, as does a window onto a garden. It was believed that man could envision things, and situate himself in their midst, independently of language. This belief was contingent upon the unquestioning acceptance of a particular model: that of a *perception* in which the perceiver and the perceived are understood to confront each other directly. All mental activity (memory, imagination, thought, and so on) was laboriously reduced to this paradigm of a direct encounter between subject and object.

Today, we say *referent* rather than *object*. "Referent" means: an object to which reference is made by means of an expression belonging to language and used in discourse. Implicit in this definition is the assumption that our access to things is mediated through language. It is this language that must be analyzed if we are to determine anything whatsoever about the relation between a person and the world.

Such is the argument we might make to convey the essence of the linguistic turn. Curiously, this argument bears a strong resemblance to that used by the old philosophy—the "philosophy of representation"—against an adversary that was, at the time, called "common sense" or "naïve realism." The "turn," then, was an "idealistic turn in philosophy."

Prior to this idealistic turn, naïve realists believed that they apprehended things directly, oblivious to the fact that things are given to us only in the representation we have of them. But the representation we have is that which we *can* have, given the constitution of our capacity to represent.

Language has replaced *representation*, but the "philosophy of representation" is perhaps not faring so badly. In any event, we can use the term "semiological hypothesis" to describe the widespread conviction that we today possess an adequate theory of the sign, a sure means of analyzing the "functioning" of "systems of signs" or of "symbolic systems."

The Semiological Hypothesis

The hypothesis is that we know today how to analyze symbolic systems. Since when have we known this? Some semiologists attribute our mastery of the symbolic to progress in the area of logic, others to progress in linguistics. In any case, our semiological science enables us to define that which is necessary in order that a group of signs function within an act of communication. It is here that the concept of the referent is introduced. Oswald Ducrot and Tzvetan Todorov provide a good definition of this concept as it is generally used in texts of a semiological orientation:

Since extra-linguistic communication often has an extra-linguistic reality as its object, a speaker must be able to designate its constituent objects: this is *the referential func-*

tion of language (the object or objects designated by an expression make up its referent). However, this reality is not necessarily *the* reality, or *the* world. Natural languages have in effect this power to construct the universe to which they refer: they can thus provide themselves with an imaginary *universe of discourse*. Treasure Island is a possible object of reference, just as is Grand Central Station.[2]

This indeed seems to be the accepted meaning of the term within the semiological school. Two particularities of this usage should be noted.

1. *An uncertainty regarding the user of the referential function.* The definition just proposed is of a hypothetical-deductive order. If, hypothetically, language exists in the service of communication, it must have a referential function because we must be able to designate referents. The referent is clearly the object designated as the object of the communicative act. But upon whom is it incumbent to do the designating? Who refers to the referent? Sometimes it is speakers who designate objects, sometimes it is natural languages that refer to a universe. (In this context, we would have to understand that, for example, the French language refers to *a* universe—necessarily one among other possibilities—and, furthermore, to a universe that it has itself constructed.)

2. *The initiation of a dialectic between outside and inside.* "Extra-linguistic reality" is not necessarily reality plain and simple. It is the outside reality *of* the sequence of language under consideration rather than

[2] Oswald Ducrot and Tzvetan Todorov, *Encyclopedic Dictionary of the Sciences of Language* (Baltimore, Md., 1979), p. 242.

the reality *outside* the sequence in question. The sequence might be, for instance, *Treasure Island*. In the novel, reference is made to a treasure island. If we consider reality plain and simple, all we find is the material text of the novel and, outside of the text, no treasure island. This treasure island has no reality outside the novel's text, except within the novel itself. The extra-linguistic reality referred to must thus be sought not outside, where the text says it is, but inside, where the text speaks of it. That which is outside must be sought inside. That which is in fact found within is given inside as if it were outside, and so on. This dialectic is a familiar one.

The French School of Semiology

The French semiological school draws its inspiration chiefly from Ferdinand de Saussure. The word *referent*, however, is not used in the *Cours de linguistique générale*.[3] The word seems to owe its favor in France to the translation into French of various articles by Roman Jakobson, among them his 1960 article on linguistics and poetics.[4] It should be recalled that, in this text, Jakobson distinguishes five functions of language, including a referential function. Jakobson, however, indicates that his analytic model, with its five

[3] Ferdinand de Saussure, *Course in General Linguistics* (New York, 1959).

[4] Roman Jakobson, "Linguistics and Poetics"; first published in 1960, this article is reprinted in *Language and Literature* (Cambridge, Mass., 1987), pp. 62–94. The model proposed by Buhler is described in his "Die Axiomatic der Sprachwissenschaft," *Kant-Studien*, 38 (1933), 19–20.

functions, is an extension of Karl Buhler's, who in fact proposed three: *Darstellung* (corresponding to the third person), *Ausdruck* (corresponding to the first person), and *Appell* (corresponding to the second person). Buhler thus followed what today we would call a *pragmatic* model, in the sense that it was derived from the system of personal pronouns *I, you, he. Presentation, expression,* and *invocation*—this model can be expressed in a formula that distinguishes three necessary positions in any communicative act:

Someone / speaks / about something / to someone.

These three positions have more recently been labeled: addressor, referent, addressee. This formula clearly shows the necessarily relative nature of the referent: the referent corresponds to the *about something.* It is not, for instance, a flower or an island, but rather a flower that is spoken about, or an island that is mentioned somewhere.

One might ask what would happen if linguistic theory were to take another tack—one suggested, for instance, by a model such as the following:

Someone / says / something / to someone / about something.

In this configuration, the three persons of the singular are no longer sufficient to identify all the positions that must be occupied for communication to take place. The addressor, referent, and addressee are no longer adequate; there must also be a *says something.* Something must be said. This suggests that pragmatism will not suffice in all cases. The semantic conditions of a discourse cannot be reduced to a set of pragmatic instances (identify who is speaking, to whom, and so forth). It is this realization that enables us to speak of an *autonomy of grammar*.

If we nonetheless follow Buhler's pragmatic model (as he proposed it, or as it was completed by Jakobson), we are deriving our notion of the referent from our notion of the third person; *he, it*—that which is neither the source of the message nor the person to whom it is addressed. If this is the case, the referent must be conceived of in terms of a person (even if it is Emile Benveniste's "non-person," the person who cannot take part in the conversation). If it is not a person, it is a thing that can be individuated and identified.

Semiologists, however, do not speak of "the referential function of certain linguistic expressions" but rather, following Jakobson's example, of the referential function of language. For Jakobson, the five linguistic functions are attached to the totality of the message; specifically, the referential function corresponds to "the message's orientation toward the context."

Here again we encounter the difficulty mentioned previously: of what is the referent the referent? A moment ago, the possibilities were: of the speaker or of the language. Now they are: of certain expressions of the language (specifically, those that can be substituted for the personal pronouns and that are sometimes called "designators"), or of the message in its entirety.

The Analysis of Language

Let us consider the following message:

Caesar crossed the Rubicon.

What is its referent? In other words, to what in this message is the referential function of language attached? To the subject of the sentence? The referent would then be Caesar. To the whole sentence? The referent would then be an event: the crossing of the Rubicon by Caesar. These answers are *logically* different, which means that they correspond to two logically distinct concepts of the "referent." The word *Caesar* is a name, a designation. If this proper name refers to anything whatsoever, it must do so in conformity with the logic of proper names. Yet the event of Caesar's crossing the Rubicon, if it is the referent of anything at all, is not the referent of a name or a designation. The event is not *designated*, but rather *signified* by means of a nominalization of the initial message. To speak of an event (and thereby make it an object of discourse), one must start with a narrative proposition (for example, *Caesar crossed the Rubicon*) and change it into a name-like phrase (by adding, for example, *the fact that* to the beginning of the original sentence).

The difference between these two notions of the referent is thus the same as that between the logic of the name and the logic of the proposition.

1. The "referent" of the message is Julius Caesar if the word "Caesar" in the message is used, in the lan-

guage of the message, to designate someone, and if that someone is Julius Caesar.

2. The "referent" of the message is the event of Caesar's crossing the Rubicon, not if these words are used to designate an event and that event is the one indicated, but rather if the sentence is true.

These two analyses are not in competition with each other. The second presupposes the first. In general, determining the reference of a linguistic expression is part of its logical analysis. In fact, the beginning of wisdom, in matters of logical analysis, is the realization that a sentence does not have *one and only one* logical form. Nothing prevents us from analyzing it sometimes one way, sometimes another. All we can legitimately require is that the analyses be compatible (for want of which the proposition will have to be rejected as equivocal).

It can be said that the message given as an example has, among other functions, that of referring us to Caesar. Yes, the message refers to Caesar if it is part of a biography of Caesar. But this does not prevent it from also referring us to the Rubicon: the sentence might be included in a summary of facts about the river. The referents of the message might well be both Caesar and the Rubicon, as in a more general history taking into account the fates of both Caesar and the Rubicon.

It is normal that several analyses be possible. It is true *of Caesar* that he crossed the Rubicon; it is true *of the Rubicon* that Caesar crossed it; it is true *of Caesar* and *of the Rubicon* that the first crossed the second; it is true *of the crossing* that this is what Caesar did in regard to the Rubicon; and all of these things are true, finally, because it is true *that* Caesar crossed the Rubicon. If it were false, it might be because the proper name *Caesar* referred to no one, or because the proper name *Rubicon* referred to nothing, or because the narrative was untrue. (Note that it is utterly futile to talk in terms of an "imaginary referent" or of the "construction of reality.")

If this is true, it must be admitted that a message's referent is something relatively indeterminate. The referent is not fixed once and for all but depends on the context of the sentence (a history of Caesar, a history of the Rubicon, a history of Rome, a history of coups d'état, and so forth). This is true, but why is the referent so nebulous?

It would be a mistake at this point to indulge in any *dialectic of the Other*, since that would fatally color our understanding of the relation between language and reality. This dialectic establishes itself all too easily as soon as we begin to talk *about* language as such in its relation to reality as such, forgetting that we started out with a simple sentence. Language would not be language if there were not something else besides language; language is thus the language of the Other of language (objective genitive). The Other of language would not be the Other of language if it depended on language. But the Other of language would depend on language if it were only that—that is, if it were that which language requires outside of itself in order to be language. But this Other of language required by language is not the simple non-language relative to language that does in effect depend on the po-

sition of language; it is, rather, an authentic and absolute Other. Conclusion: the Other supposed by
language is that which supposes itself in a language
of the Other (subjective genitive). We can easily recognize here a Fichtean exercise of the Self and the
non-Self. But this sort of dialectic need not emerge at
all. If the referent of a message is problematic, it is
quite simply because the referent has been defined as
being "what a message is about," and this very notion
of "what a message is about" is imprecise.[5]

The Original Misconception of the
Notion of the Referent

The current common usage of the term "referent"
may well have been introduced by G. K. Ogden and
I. A. Richards in *The Meaning of Meaning*.[6] This work
celebrated the advent of a science of symbolism. The
authors proposed the now-famous triangle whose
apexes were labeled: *symbol, reference,* and *referent.*
These three technical terms replaced the three more
commonplace words that made up the title of the first
chapter: "Thoughts, Words and Things." Ogden and
Richards explained in a note why they chose the English word *referent*: "It seemed desirable . . . to intro-
duce a technical term to stand for whatever we may
be thinking of or referring to" (p. 9).

Referent, they indicate, will therefore replace
terms such as *thing, object, entity, ens.* It should be

5 Nelson Goodman, "About," *Mind,* 70 (1961), 1–24; reprinted in Nelson Goodman, *Problems and Projects* (New York, 1972).
6 G. K. Ogden and I. A. Richards, *The Meaning of Meaning* (New York,
1923).

emphasized that, at the time of their writing, the translation of Gottlob Frege's term *Bedeutung* by *reference* had not yet been proposed. When, in the same work, Ogden and Richards mention Frege's distinction between *Sinn* and *Bedeutung*, they follow Bertrand Russell's distinction between *meaning* for *Sinn* and *indication* for *Bedeutung* (p. 274).[7]

The constitutive flaw in the theory of the referent proposed in *The Meaning of Meaning* is obvious. It becomes apparent even in the diagram given by the authors on page 11:

THOUGHT OR REFERENCE

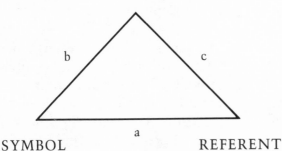

SYMBOL   a   REFERENT

where side a is labeled *Stands for (true)*, side b is labeled *Symbolizes (correct)*, and side c is labeled *Refers to (adequate)*. In other words, the symbol replaces or *stands for* a referent (and this symbol is true if it is, in fact, the one that corresponds to the referent for which it is being used). The symbol *symbolizes* a

---

[7] As a translation for *Bedeutung*, *indication* is peculiar, but *reference* is also problematic; on this point, consult M. Black and P. Geach, "Glossary," in *Translations from the Philosophical Writings of Gottlob Frege* (Oxford, 1980), and M. Dummet, *The Interpretation of Frege's Philosophy* (London, 1981).

thought, correctly or incorrectly. Finally, the thought *refers to* the referent, adequately or inadequately.

If we confine ourselves to this diagram, it seems natural to conclude that the symbol in question is propositional in nature. The referent in the diagram will thus be the fact corresponding to the particular clause. This is precisely what is suggested by an example given later in the book (p. 62): I strike a match and I expect that match to light. My expectation consists of a certain "thought," which can be "symbolized" by a "symbol," specifically, the sentence *the match will light*. This symbol will be true if the match does in fact light, and false if the match does not light. In this example, the symbol is propositional and the referent is a fact.

However, the example given by Ogden and Richards immediately after their diagram is quite different. In this example, the symbol is the word *Napoleon*, the referent is the Emperor Napoleon, and the reference is the *idea* of Napoleon. Here, the symbol is a proper name and the referent is an individual. Hence we find again the common understanding of something like "the object of reference" meant in the sense of: that about which one is speaking in a singular proposition whose subject is a *proper name*. But if we try to apply the concepts established in the diagram to this example, we end up with absurd results. Granted, we can label the apexes of the triangle: Napoleon's name, Napoleon the person, and the idea of Napoleon. So far, so good. But the sides of the triangle become unintelligible. It would be necessary for the name *Napoleon* to be true or untrue of Napoleon.

How can a proper name be true or false? There appears to be total confusion here between naming and predicating. If we could say that the word *Napoleon* were true of the individual Napoleon, we should be able to say, for the same reason, that the word *Talleyrand* is untrue of Napoleon. Now, we happen to know that Napoleon was not a liberal. The predicate *is liberal* is therefore untrue of Napoleon. If *is liberal* is untrue of Napoleon, it follows that the predicate *is not liberal* is true of Napoleon. But if we were able to say that the name *Talleyrand* was untrue of Napoleon, we ought to be able to say that the name *non-Talleyrand* is true of Napoleon. Inversely, if Napoleon cannot be designated by using the expression *non-Talleyrand*, it is because it is absurd to qualify the relation between the name and the named entity with the adjectives *true* or *false*.

The Semiological Apologue of the Cloakroom

This fundamental misconception of the referent has its counterpart in an equally longstanding misconception of the sign itself. People speak about the sign, but we are never told whether the science of signs (or of sign systems) is dealing with signs in the sense of symbols that "stand for" something (and thus with the sign as name), or rather with signs in the sense of their being what one uses to signify, to say something. The quandaries of the referent are thus also very much the quandaries of the sign. The first tenet of the semiological hypothesis seems to be that the sign replaces the thing: *the symbol stands for a referent.* This assumption informs not only the work of Ogden and Richards, but also, if his remark cited below is indicative, Jakobson's theories of the sign: "Modern structuralist thought has clearly established the fact that language is a system of signs; linguistics is an integral part of the science of signs, *semiotics* (or, in Saussurean terms, *semiology*). Our era has resurrected the medieval definition of the sign—*aliquid stat pro aliquo*—and shown it to be valid and fruitful."[8]

Thus, wherever something stands for something else, there is a sign. This "definition" of the sign (which invites us to equate signification and substitution) favors the following observation: signs enable us to designate and describe things that are absent in the here and now. Proper names make it possible to refer to absent people and distant places. They enable us to apply the predicative system of language to what happens not here but elsewhere, not today but in another time, and so on.

It is in this context that a particular sophism came to play a decisive role: signs are indispensable when we wish to communicate about things that are absent, *therefore* signs are useless when it comes to dealing with things that are present—or at least signs would be useless if the things signified were really present.

The immediate consequence of this: *Since* in fact signs are useful and even indispensable in all com-

8 Roman Jakobson, "L'Aspect phonologique et l'aspect grammatical du langage dans leurs interrelations," in *Essais de linguistique générale* (Paris, 1963), p. 162.

munication, whether their subject is absent or present in the setting of the conversation, *therefore* things are never truly present.

A statement of the sophism: The use of signs is necessary to represent that which is absent; *therefore* the absence of that which the sign signifies is necessary to any use of signs.

One more step and we end up with Hegel's famous dictum, on which Alexandre Koyré, Alexandre Kojève, Jean Hyppolite, Maurice Blanchot, Jacques Lacan,[9] and so many others have commented:

The word is the murder of the thing.

Semiological theory has multiplied the paradoxes surrounding the referent. One might say of these paradoxes exactly what Freud said of delirium. For the people around the madman, the outbreak of delirium is the signal of madness; it is the best proof of an actual derangement. But, continues Freud, this symptom is also the hallmark of improvement, for the madman's delirium reveals his desire to be cured, a desire that expresses itself in his "corrected" reconstruction of reality. In much the same way, the paradoxes of the referent are semiology's delirium; they, too, are efforts to correct a model that was aberrant from the beginning. Each such paradox represents an

9 See Alexandre Koyré, "Hegel à Iéna," in *Etudes d'histoire de la pensée philosophique* (Paris, 1961); Alexandre Kojève, *Introduction to the Reading of Hegel* (New York, 1969); Jean Hyppolite, *Logique et existence: Essai sur la logique de Hegel* (Paris, 1953); Maurice Blanchot, *La Part du feu* (Paris, 1949); and Jacques Lacan, *Séminaire I: Sur les écrits techniques de Freud* (Paris, 1975).

additional contortion imposed on a model substitut-
ing the sign for the referent, in order that the model
might somehow meet the demands made upon it—
that is to say, so that it might furnish us with an adequate explanation of the workings of semiotic systems. There comes a time, however, when the model
has been so thoroughly corrected and twisted that it
cancels itself out.

The following apologue will allow us to follow the
strange fate of the semiological model. Let us say that
signs are like the chits given out in a cloakroom. The
"cloakroom system" works in the following way: in
exchange for your overcoat, you are given a chit identified by a number corresponding to the hanger on
which your overcoat will be hung. By pure convention, this chit represents your overcoat. The main features of the system are as follows:

1. The association between the chit and the overcoat is *arbitrary*. One cannot wear a chit, nor can one
put an overcoat in one's pocket.

2. The chit is, as we might expect, *the murder of
the overcoat*. When the cloakroom system is functioning as it should, I cannot have both my chit and
my overcoat—the sign and the thing itself—at the
same time. If I have my coat, it means either that I
haven't yet received my chit or that I have already returned it. If I have my chit, I am entitled to a coat.

3. A distinction must be made between the *dia-
chronic* and *synchronic* points of view. Prior to the exchange of a particular overcoat for a particular chit,
no relation existed between the two. All there was in
the "treasury of the cloakroom" was a reserve of chits,

all different and *all diacritical*, but none predestined
to take the place of such and such an overcoat. When
the exchange of overcoats for chits has taken place, a
certain state of the system becomes fixed (and it will
be revised each time an overcoat is reclaimed by its
owner). After the exchange, a certain assimilation
takes place between the chit and the overcoat. If this
chit takes the place of my coat, I will be as attached
to the chit as I was to my coat. As long as the coat remains in the cloakroom, the chit is a pledge of my
coat, the promise that it will be returned to me.

Such is the cloakroom system when it is functioning normally. Within its normal functioning, this system is incapable of representing the workings of language as such. At most, this model represents a kind
of language game that is one possible game among
many others.

Suppose, however, that we wished to defend a definition of the linguistic sign as a substitute or as a
chit. To do this, we would have to modify the cloakroom to reflect many obvious aspects of human language: the cloakroom would have to become paradoxical.

First, we would have to ask why the chit is assumed
to be the symbol of the overcoat, and not the opposite.
What is there to prevent us from seeing the overcoats
as symbols and the chits as referents? Answer: there
is, in principle, nothing to prevent this. The cloakroom chit is the symbol of the overcoat because, as it
happens, we attach more value to overcoats than we
do to chits in and of themselves. Now let us imagine
a tyrannical cloakroom attendant who decides she is

no longer going to return coats in exchange for chits. The chits would no longer be convertible but would be totally devalued, like Russian bonds. Or, in an inverse scenario, suppose that, following some fashion crush, the chits from a particularly chic cloakroom came to be admired and hoarded by collectors. In this case, one can imagine aficionados rushing to exchange their ratty overcoats for one of the precious chits.

The conclusion we are forced to draw is that, in a system of substitutions like that of the cloakroom, nothing predestines certain things to serve as symbols and others to serve as referents. There is, therefore, no *ultimate referent* in the sense of something that can be obtained through an exchange but that can, in itself, no longer be exchanged for something else. Only empirical considerations dictate that we stop with the exchange of the overcoat for the chit. Neither does there exist any *ultimate word*. There is no last word, no word of all words, with which we might obtain the ultimate referent. We must therefore begin to speak of a *nihilism of the cloakroom*. Nothing exists that cannot be exchanged; there is nothing such that one would not or could not exchange it "for anything in the world." All things can become chits. All things can be established as substitutable for something else. This brand of nihilism is not in fact a radical philosophical reversal, but merely one property of the model adopted here to describe symbolization.

Nothing escapes symbolization, nothing escapes a trip to the cloakroom—except, perhaps, such metaphysical words as *nothing* and *something, nothingness* and *being*. It is true that, in the cloakroom, there is no ultimate referent, unless it be by habit or convention. All things can become signs. There is no ultimate word, no sign of an ultimate referent or, if one does not distinguish between signified and referent, no sign of a "transcendental signified." Unless, that is, we take the words *nothing* and *something* as chits of a different order. They are signs, and therefore chits, but they are metaphysical chits. The *nothing* chit will be exchanged in the cloakroom for: nothing. The *something* chit will be exchanged in the cloakroom for: again, nothing. For if, in the cloakroom, I was given *just any* overcoat in exchange for the *something* chit, I would at the same time be receiving a specific overcoat that corresponded to a specific chit, and that chit would then be deprived of its referent.

The model must undergo a second correction if we are to represent language as a symbolic system—in other words, as a system of chits. The cloakroom could no longer function if people were to receive a chit without surrendering an overcoat or to recover an overcoat without returning a chit. The substitutions of chits and overcoats are perfectly defined. On this point, the assimilation between cloakroom chits and linguistic signs breaks down. Each speaker has symbols at his disposal, but how did he acquire them? What have I given up in exchange for the words given to me? Have I, for instance, somewhere deposited the "things" whose "names" I know? I do not remember any such exchange. According to the semiological conception of language, we are a bit like people waking up the morning after a rough night about which we remember nothing. We find mysterious cloak-room tickets in our pockets. We do not know where we received these tickets, nor what we exchanged for them. If I have a ticket, I have the right to a corre-sponding exchange that is corollary to the first ex-change from which I saved the ticket. It is sufficient to know that the ticket is a ticket. I can thus use sym-bols without having the least idea of the referents cor-responding to them.

How, then, might we conceive of *the origin of lan-guage*—in other words, of the episode during which we received our first chits? Two versions of this epi-sode might be suggested. The first claims to be posi-tive; the second admits to being allegorical.

The positive version. Symbols were acquired dur-ing the language-learning process. Since I do not re-member it, this prehistoric event must be recon-structed by reasoning out what must have taken place. That an exchange did take place is the very sub-stance of the semiological hypothesis: the signs are chits. It is hard to see how this exchange could have taken place as we learned a specific word. To learn a specific word, one must first have acquired the lan-guage. We must therefore go back to the learning of a "first word" or, better still, to the origin of the sym-bolic faculty itself. The *first chit* is a word that can be exchanged for anything whatsoever; it is our very fac-ulty of effecting an exchange in the form of a babylike babbling that is in the process of becoming articu-lated language. What has been given up in exchange for this ability to exchange? The alternative of *not* effecting an exchange, of *not* using the cloakroom. In the initial exchange, therefore, one gives up the ability to not exchange, to not make a trip to the cloakroom. The initial exchange is the one in which we give up the power to not exchange in order to receive the chits that will be the necessary currency of all future exchanges.

The way is now open to psychologize this structuralist schema: we might call the (imaginary) power not to exchange "phallic power," the fact of escaping the laws of the semiotic cloakroom "incest," and the ordeal of exchange "castration." In an unabashedly psychological version of the scenario, we would not hesitate to say that the ultimate referent of all exchanges is none other than the lost paradise of possessing all the women within the group. As concerns a psychology of the child, this woman is the mother. In the ethnologist's eyes, she would be, rather, the daughter or the sister. This is, moreover, unimportant: if the wife takes the place of the incestuous object, that object itself refers back to nothing. Everything signifies it, but it signifies nothing.

The allegorical version. In fact, the story of the origin of language cannot be told, except in a fable. Even the so-called positive version cannot avoid making use of an image, of an "as if" in the conditional. A subtler strategy would be to give a figurative version of events—that is, to frankly concede that our story is only a tale or a manner of speaking about things that are in fact not like our representations of them.

The original exchange of the *thing itself* for the

word never took place. Nothing has been left behind in the cloakroom. Chits were not given out in exchange for an object to be held. The chits are things, like others, that one uses to represent other things, which themselves replace still others, and so on ad infinitum. There is no thing itself, no ultimate thing. Everything is, in one way or another, *in the place* of another thing. The thing itself, if it existed, would be that which stood for nothing and existed in perfect self-sufficiency. Therefore we have left nothing behind, lost nothing. Nonetheless, signs are chits (a fact that the semiological hypothesis would not dream of questioning). Thus we cannot help but conceive of language as having symbolically replaced things themselves. The very nature of language inevitably gives rise to this illusion, this "transcendental appearance." Hence the sign is that which stands for something else; a thing that is not a sign is that which stands for nothing. The thing is *always already* lost. This loss has always already taken place, meaning that it has never happened in the present. The chits we hold in our hands bear the memory of this primordial exchange; they are the *traces* of an exchange that "will have taken place." They are the pledges of a restitution that has been due since the beginning. Meanwhile, in the interlude between the lost paradise and the awaited parousia, there is only the reign of an endless circulation of signs.

To say "transcendental appearance" is necessarily to call for a critique of this concept. If the hypothesis of originary substitution were a theoretical error committed by certain semiologists, it could be corrected. But if this hypothesis is inevitable, if it is integral to all "theories of the sign," then the critique of semiology must be a critique of language (just as, if the sophisms of that metaphysics are inevitable illusions, the critique of rational metaphysics must also be a critique of pure reason). The critique of language directly concerns the illusion of the referent: the illusion of something that must bring together the two attributes by which the thing itself is defined, specifically:

1. That it serve as the referent of a sign.
2. That it not serve as sign for another referent.

As we can see, the *critique of pure language* remains very much justified so long as the illusion of a possible exchange between language as a whole and reality as a whole is a necessary error of the human mind.

I have tried in this essay to suggest that the illusion of an *ultimate referent* of *language per se*—of what dialecticians call the Other of language—is not a transcendental appearance. If the preceding remarks are justified, the illusion in question reflects, instead, the inadequacy of the chosen paradigm. At the origin of this illusion there is nothing that is necessary, only a cascade of *reductions*. All signs have been treated as words. All words have been treated as names. All names have been treated as symbols. What must be critiqued is not so much "language" or "the symbolic function" as it is the longstanding indifference of our contemporary theoreticians toward what grammarians call the division of the *parts of speech*.

Reality and the Untheorizable

Clément Rosset

Apart from a few isolated thinkers such as Lucretius, Spinoza, or Nietzsche, as well as Montaigne and the nominalist philosophers Abelard and Occam, the notion of reality plays only the most insignificant role in our philosophical systems and problematics. Reality as such is generally not taken into account. It is called into service only on those occasions when it is a question of refuting fallacious reasoning, of denouncing the frequent misfires of intellectual speculation—and even then, little thought is given to actually defining its status. It is in the name of reality that we triumphantly settle our accounts with error, illusion, imagination, dream, fantasy, and desire. But its role stops there. Whereas we frequently encounter the question of a discrepancy from the real, very little is said of the real itself from which we happen to diverge. The formal teaching of philosophy gives only the shortest shrift to the idea of reality. It is interesting to note, for example, that reality is not on the list of philosophical topics making up the program of either past or present French baccalaureate examinations. Including reality

in the list of officially recognized philosophical notions would doubtless produce, to the eyes of some, a
slightly incongruous effect: somewhat like including,
between the notions of reason and liberty, those of pot
roast or cheese.

Two main reasons are generally given to explain the
origin of this philosophical rejection of the notion of
reality. In the first place, reality is seen as an eminently dubious notion consisting only of the endless
and forever contradictory sum of the diverse observations we make of it. There are as many different perceptions as there are points of view. "To each his own
reality," we might say, modifying only slightly the title of Pirandello's well-known litany of relativism.
Moreover, this same reality offers itself to the individual observer only through the intermediary of perception and the senses, whose fidelity and reliability
are easily challenged. This raises a doubt regarding
the nature of reality as it is perceived by each of us,
and with that comes the other litany, even more ancient, of the errors of the senses.

In the second place, reality is seen as something eminently devoid of interest. On the one hand, it is made
up of objects that are transient and therefore derisory.
On the other, these same objects, in addition to being
marked by the flaw of the ephemeral, are repetitive
and banal—a twofold quality that, in the eyes of lucid
but sad thinkers, would assimilate the real to that su-
preme evil of everything that is without duration and
without newness. The meagerness and banality of the
real is, we know, a theme illustrated not only by the
history of philosophy but also, and even more abun-

dantly, by the history of literature, especially romantic and post-romantic literature. A famous remark by Rimbaud sums up the first grievance: "La vraie vie est absente." And another, by Jules Laforgue, summarizes the second: "Ah! Que la Vie est quotidienne."

One might point to a contradiction here (but, as we will see, only an apparent contradiction) between these two objections to reality. The flaws they confirm—that of being unknowable and that of being everyday—in fact establish reality as something that is simultaneously too mysterious and not mysterious enough, too indiscernible to be known but too banal to be interesting.

The following remarks are intended to defend a position that is very much opposed to these objections. They propose to establish: (1) that the obscurity of the notion of reality, as well as the disappointment that that obscurity normally entails, result neither from the relativity of our points of view nor from the weaknesses of our perception, but rather from the *singular* constitution of reality itself; (2) that the objection to the meagerness and banality of reality is not in opposition to the difficulty of knowing it, but is an inevitable or at least logical consequence of that difficulty; and finally, (3) that these objections to reality imply a philosophical prejudice (a conviction about the intrinsic insufficiency of reality) to which we would oppose our own conviction about the intrinsic sufficiency of reality. Following Leibnitz's famous "principle of sufficient reason," I shall call this conviction the *principle of sufficient reality*.

Reality and Disappointment

If the notion of reality has not managed to "break through" in the history of philosophy, if it has failed and continues to fail to arouse philosophical interest, this is first and foremost because it has never been able to impose itself as a *notion*. There has never been a notion of reality, and the principal value of a reflection on reality lies, paradoxically, in our philosophical incapacity to establish for it any fixed definition. A notion may of course be called into question, but for all critical and philosophical purposes, it must also be capable of being described and defined. To so define it, we need both a temporal distance from it (if we are to analyze the facts on which it is based) and a spatial distance from it (if we are to be in a position to observe those facts). This spatio-temporal distance, which in classical Greece characterized the ideas of both study and leisure (*scholē*), is a necessary precondition to all reflection and to all philosophy. Reality, however, refuses us all such distance. Its immediacy frustrates every possibility of reflection. It is like a meteor that goes undetected by the observational devices aimed at it because it passes too quickly and too nearby. Occurring right here and right now, it allows—like that cruelest of all realities, death itself— neither delay nor distance.

It is not enough to say that reality presents itself to us under the auspices of urgency. It is more urgent than any urgency. Reality does not allow even that instant of delay (usually insignificant and useless, given the lack of time) that normally separates our perception of a critical situation from the perception of measures appropriate to cope with it. Faced with reality, thought is caught short, inevitably disconcerted and discountenanced. The experience of reality—to the extent we can speak here of experience (and we will see later that this is possible in a certain sense)—is thus comparable to the experience of that ambiguous gaiety Nietzsche speaks of in *The Case of Wagner* when he refers to Bizet's *Carmen*: "This music is gay; but not in a French or German way. Its gaiety is African. Fate hangs over it. Its happiness is short, sudden, and without pardon."[1] Nietzsche's observation is valid for all reality, whether we perceive it as gay or sad. We know, moreover, that this quality of being "without pardon" (*ohne Pardon*), which Nietzsche appropriately attributes to the cruel gaiety of Bizet's music in *Carmen*, is, in current usage, more usually associated with a disastrous event or decision. Happiness and sadness share the fate common to our every experience of reality—namely, that of being immediate but only immediate. And the "fatality" that hovers over reality does not, as Nietzsche points out, imply that it is the result of some predetermined destiny, but only that its immediacy renders it both inescapable in terms of its instantaneous appearance and more than uncertain with respect to its chances for duration or survival. The inescapable, we must remember, does not designate that which is necessary

[1] Friedrich Nietzsche, *The Case of Wagner*, in *The Complete Works of Friedrich Nietzsche*, trans. Anthony M. Ludovici, vol. 8 (London, 1911), p. 3.

from all eternity, but that from which it is impossible to escape in this very instant.

This immediacy of the real has two major consequences. The first consequence is that our perception of reality has the particular characteristic of in no way contributing to the formation of an experience. We must, of course, agree here on what we mean by experience. If by this term we mean a wisdom accumulated as the result of our abortive "experiences" of reality, a knowledge that grows every day more certain of its status as something fleeting and testing (testing in the sense of being probative and decisive in the last instance—or rather in the first instance, since they are one and the same), then it is obvious that we can legitimately speak of an experience of reality in much the same way that we speak, for instance, of an experience of life or of a knowledge of wines. But if we mean by experience a recognition of something that remains the same and a "getting used to" the real, then properly speaking there can be no such thing as an experience of the real, any more than there can be, as already indicated, any experimenting with it in the sense of scientific observation.

The real is the only thing in the world we can never get used to. I have said this elsewhere[2] in ways that will probably be taken as indulgences in paradox or jest—insinuating, in effect, that there are many things that are not real and, moreover, that it is far easier to get used to the unreal than to the real. Here, however, it is a case neither of paradox nor of jest. Our

[2] See Clément Rosset, *Le Réel et son double* (Paris, 1976) and *Le Réel: Traité de l'idiotie* (Paris, 1977).

everyday experience teaches us clearly that the human mind, although it often must struggle to put up with things that exist, grows quite easily accustomed to and even takes pleasure in things that do not exist. The reason for this apparently paradoxical proclivity is that reality itself is far too changeable ever to allow us to get used to it in any sense. Yet the representations that we might extrapolate from the real are more than sufficiently stable for us to become used to them, and even to draw from them the basis of an idée fixe. This effect of habituation—so perceptible, for example, in our experience of medicines and drugs, or in our observation of what is supposedly repetitive in certain aspects of the normal—is powerless against the perception of a reality grasped outside the normal, of a reality that, because of the virulence and precision either of its specific instant or of its specific place, becomes a "moment of truth."

There is no "getting used to" a reality that by its very nature frustrates our every attempt to anticipate its awaited outcome. The domain of reality is that vast domain of everything it is impossible to anticipate. It is an *unhabitual* domain by its very essence, one perhaps recognized as such by Empedocles in an enigmatic fragment of his *Songs of Purification*: "I cried and I sobbed at the sight of that unfamiliar dwelling." It is certainly a banal domain to the eyes of those who, probably like Plato and certainly like many of those he inspired (including Kierkegaard), would assimilate a repetition of the unforeseeable to a repetition of the same and, in so doing, make of what is perpetually new something that is perpetually boring. This is done either out of boredom with what changes or out of what might be called a habit of the unhabitual. But reality is a domain forever new to the eyes of those who, like Lucretius, adopt a contrary point of view: "But no, everything is new in this world, everything is recent" (*De rerum natura*, V, 330).

The second consequence is that our perception of reality becomes something meager and uninformative because it is limited to itself, because it can neither justify nor enrich itself through any other *image* of reality. What makes reality confused is neither the multiplicity nor the divergence of our points of view on it, but rather the absence of any *useful* point of view. If reality eludes reflection, it is not only because it is immediate but because it is singular, unique, and consequently cannot be captured in any mirror that might reflect its image. Reality is precisely that of which we can never perceive a double except in fantasy or illusion. It consists only of itself and constitutes, as Ernst Mach would put it, a unilateral being whose mirror image cannot exist. This absence of any mirror image establishes reality as an object that is only half observable and half knowable—like an inside of which we can never know the outside (and vice versa), or like an "idiocy" when we take that word to mean, following the original sense of the Greek *idiōtēs*, a singularity without replica. It is for this reason that the theme of the *double* (or, more exactly, that of the missing double) has always haunted the problematic of the real like its longed-for yet absent shadow. It is like the invisible city of Kitèje in the Rimsky-Korsakov opera, which doubles the material and transient Kitèje. What is fundamentally disappointing about reality, and what makes it a disagreeable object, even a "disagreeing" object, is the way it offers itself without the guarantee of any sort of double that might, in the modern commercial sense of the word, "insure" it by covering its expenses in the case of an accident or by replacing it in the event of loss. Thus it is that Oedipus, in the legend illustrated by Sophocles' play, loses himself and all his possessions for having failed to write into the contract binding him to the kingdom of Thebes, a contract in which he promises to find and punish the murderer of the city's former prince, a restrictive clause excluding his own person. When he discovers himself to be flagrantly guilty of the crime of which he so indiscriminately suspected all the others, he can extricate himself from the difficulty only by considering himself as an other, by effecting a fantasmatic distinction between the Oedipus he is and the murderer he seeks. He finds a way out that is necessary yet impossible, and that defines unquestionably both the tragic character of his own destiny and that of all reality in general. The trap Oedipus finds himself caught in is that of all reality: coinciding with itself, it offers neither the alternative nor the possibility of any double.

The Devaluation of the Real

Faced with such an impasse, the temptation is to designate the real as something insufficient and unsatisfying on both an intellectual and an affective level, to oppose to it the idea of "another reality" that is somehow more real than the reality we actually perceive. Thus it was that Eric Weil, in his article "De la réalité," could write that the "real reality" is not that which is given to us in immediate experience: "What is immediately given to us is not real."[3] Such a statement might, of course, seem mad, and it undoubtedly is, at least to a certain extent. However, this distinction between a "real reality" and a "perceived reality" is quite ancient and can even be said to constitute one of the classic oppositions running through the history of philosophy. The distinctions made by Plato between the perceptible and the intelligible, by Hegel between rational reality and empirical reality, and by Heidegger between Being and beings are only the best-known formulations of this differentiation. We could easily add to them more modern formulations, such as Jacques Lacan's distinction between the symbolic and the real, Jacques Derrida's claim that all metaphysics is only an interminable variation on that same distinction, and Jean Baudrillard's formulation in *De la séduction* (which at least has the merit of being brief and of laying its cards on the table): "The real in general is the abolished and disenchanted form of the world. . . . Moreover, the real has never interested anyone."[4]

However, this devaluation of the banal real in favor of some other real that is truer and more consistent cannot be considered an altogether extravagant op-

[3] Eric Weil, "De la réalité," in *Essais et conférences* (Paris, 1970), p. 299.
[4] Jean Baudrillard, *De la séduction* (Paris, 1979), p. 69.

tion. Quite to the contrary, it constitutes a kind of "common opinion" around which, in their various ways, the majority of philosophers and writers have always rallied. It goes without saying that when I say a "common opinion," I do not mean a negligible opinion, but rather a majority opinion and therefore a quite well-considered one. Paul Eluard wrote, for example, in an issue of *La Révolution surréaliste*: "Let Raymond Roussel show us everything which has not been. For some of us it is only that reality that matters."[5] Eluard says this apparently without suspecting that the exclusive "some of us" with whom he would align himself in fact constitutes by far the greatest number. In the same way, the rejection of reality once proclaimed by André Breton did not mean what he thought it meant, quite in contrast to that height of originality and insolence he intended. His was only one more way—a way as noisy as it was unconscious—of rallying to what is by far the most common way of thinking.

The Principle of Sufficient Reality

This disqualification of the immediate real in favor of some more real or "surreal" reality implies, as already mentioned, a philosophical prejudice—a conviction about the insufficiency of immediate reality as something guilty of offering no firm hold either to reflection or to our hope for lasting happiness. To this

[5] Paul Eluard, *La Révolution surréaliste*, 4 (1925), cited in the special issue *Roussel en Sorbonne* of *Bizarre* (1964), p. 70.

philosophical prejudice we might well oppose another: a conviction about the intrinsic sufficiency of
reality, and therefore about the futility of all those exterior illuminations called up in our failed attempts
to elucidate its enigmatic singularity. Such a conviction about the sufficiency of the real is, of course, in
no way tantamount to claiming that reality is self-ex-
planatory, that it has no mysteries, that its existence
is self-evident. Our position asks only that we consider this reality, as elusive and ephemeral as it may
be, as, on the one hand, the only one there is and, on
the other, as the only one capable of making us happy.
Yet even giving reality that status (one considerably
reduced in terms of its philosophical pretentions) is
generally rejected, because it frustrates all hope of rational explanation and all possibility of an alternative
or a compromise. Hence the eternal taunts addressed
by most philosophers to those thinkers who admit to
being interested in immediate experience and even to
being satisfied with it. Hegel, for example, in that remarkable passage at the beginning of his *Phenomenology of Mind*, ranks such a state of mind below even
that of animal wisdom:

We may answer those who insist on the truth and certitude
of objects of sense by saying that they had better be sent
back to the most elementary school of wisdom, the ancient
Eleusinian mysteries of Ceres and Bacchus. They have not
yet learned the inner secret of the eating of bread and the
drinking of wine. For one who is initiated into these mysteries not only comes to doubt the being of things of sense,
but despairs of it altogether. In dealing with them he partly

brings about the nothingness of these things, partly he sees these bring about their own nothingness. Even animals are not shut off from this wisdom, but show they are deeply initiated into it. They do not stand stock still before things of sense as if these were things *per se*: they despair of this reality altogether, and in complete assurance of the nothingness of things, they fall to without more ado and eat them up. All nature proclaims, as animals do, these open secrets, these mysteries revealed to all which teach what the truth of things of sense is.[6]

This devalorizing of immediate reality is a particularly eloquent expression of the "principle of insufficient reality" that constitutes the credo common to all philosophical denials of the real. It is also a rather amusing expression of it because of the way Hegel suggests an equivalence between the animals' appetite and their recognition of the ontological poverty of the food they are about to devour. It is as if we first had to convince the pig of the meager reality of the swill we are offering him, of its absolute nothingness, before he would deign to set his teeth into it. It is true, however, as Hegel says, that this despairing of reality, even if it hardly explains the animals' appetite, explains very well our own lack of appetite for the real when we deplore it as something both too irrational to be thought of and too instantaneous to be negotiated. It is for this reason that the philosophical rehabilitation of the notion of reality presupposes, as I have indicated elsewhere,[7] a double and complemen-

---

[6]G. W. F. Hegel, *The Phenomenology of Mind*, trans. J. B. Baillie (London, 1949), pp. 158–59.

[7]See Clément Rosset, *Logique du pire* (Paris, 1971).

tary condition: that of a blind love for life and that of a certain knowledge of its tragic character—tragic because it is irremediable.

If my suggesting the expression "principle of sufficient reality" as a motto for this rehabilitation of the real is uncommon, the philosophical option it designates is nonetheless not entirely new, even though it is relatively rare in the field of philosophy. This principle constitutes, in fact, the very keystone of the three philosophical systems to which I referred at the beginning of this essay: those of Lucretius, Spinoza (who, in his *Ethics*, likens the idea of reality to that of perfection), and Nietzsche. But such systems are rare, and they are ordinarily accepted as philosophical only to the extent that this idea of a sufficient reality is separated out from them and treated as something scandalous and absurd, despite the fact that it is the centerpiece of these systems. Such is the case for Nietzsche, who was considered by Heidegger and is even today considered by Heidegger's disciples only insofar as they ignore his fundamental refutation of all metaphysical or ontological theses. They ignore, for instance, that passage from *The Twilight of the Idols* where Nietzsche states:

The characteristics with which man has endowed the "true being" of things are the characteristics of non-being, of *nothingness*. The "true world" has been erected upon a contradiction of the real world. It is indeed an apparent world, seeing that it is merely a moralo-optical delusion. . . . There is no sense in spinning yarns about another world, provided, of course, that we do not possess a mighty instinct which urges us to slander, belittle, and cast suspicion upon this life.[8]

It is no doubt surprising but certainly worthy of note that, despite their often attentive and even meticulous readings of his texts, none of Nietzsche's modern interpreters has yet succeeded in correctly deciphering the meaning of a message that is, nonetheless, so clear.

'Under the Volcano'

In Malcolm Lowry's *Under the Volcano*, the Consul walks with no precise goal, in no determined direction, and with a step that is at the same time both uncertain and sure. An incurable drunk, he has already been imbibing valiantly, despite the early morning hour, to celebrate the return of his ex-wife Yvonne, whom he had been waiting for at the Quauhnahuac bar (the chance to have a few more glasses). They will return to the Consul's villa on foot. Let's get on with it, and try to make a good impression. With Yvonne at his side, the Consul pulls it off and somehow manages to place one foot in front of the other, all the while talking with a touch of solemnity "as somehow, anyhow, they moved on."[9] Somehow, anyhow; that is to say: anyhow, somehow.

The day promises to be long and hard. A thousand trials await the Consul before this evening of the Feast

[8] Friedrich Nietzsche, *The Twilight of the Idols*, in *The Complete Works of Friedrich Nietzsche*, trans. Anthony M. Ludovici, vol. 16 (London, 1911), p. 22.

[9] Malcolm Lowry, *Under the Volcano* (New York, 1947), p. 60.

of the Dead, when he himself will find death. But they are trials from which he will emerge victorious (except for the last one), thanks to the persistence of an alcoholic, semi-comatose state that puts him out of reach, so to speak. The first obstacle will come early in the morning, when he meets an overzealous compatriot who worries at seeing him asleep on the roadside and innocently offers a flask of whiskey to help him get back on his feet: the Consul will quickly get through this one. Back at the villa, Yvonne, who has washed and waits for him in her room, will hardly cause him any more problems. A deep and much-needed siesta at the edge of the pool, where he is subject to strange hallucinations, will offer him another temporary escape (it is only eight in the morning, and things can wait). A short time later the Consul will courageously escape the scathing reprimands of a neighbor who is not about to be taken in and who directly asks him the right question: "You're doing *what*?" After that, he escapes as best he can his bouts of nausea on the "maquina infernal" of the Quauhnahuac carnival. He escapes getting involved at the Cantina del Bosque, where he stands next to Señora Gregorio, just as he will escape the *toros* at Tomalin, the mirages of the Salon Ofelia, and the questions asked by the dubious officers in the Farolito bar at Parian, who would force him to join the Mexican Police: he would make an excellent informer. Sensing a vague danger in the insistence of these men, the Consul flees; but the drunken policemen, none too happy at being treated so impolitely, quickly catch up with him. They kill him and throw his body into the large ravine at the foot of the city, the ravine into which so many things have already fallen.

To get to this point, much energy and determination are called for, and the Consul is lacking in neither. Behind the protection of his dark glasses, and helping himself along when need be with a strong cane, the Consul knows where he is going and will not be intimidated. His is the admirable willpower not only of someone who wants nothing but also of someone who, if he did want something, would be incapable of being aware of it. We know that, in his *Discourse on Method*, Descartes recommends always forging straight ahead if we at least want to be sure of arriving somewhere. Strengthened by this certitude, the Consul does not hesitate and follows his path fully awake, fully lucid, fully capable of facing whatever might cross his path. The fact is that he will not miss a single step on the itinerary that leads him, from cantina to cantina, all the way to the *barranca*, the ravine of death.

And how could it be otherwise? Why shouldn't the road he follows in so apparently muddled a fashion be precisely his route, the one he wanted and chose? "Whatever I do, I will do it deliberately," says the Consul. He is right. Where there is a will, there is, as we say, a way. But the opposite is also true: where there is a way, you can always find a will. After the fact it is always possible to imagine a will that ties together a succession of insignificant actions, in the same way that Leibniz's omniscient God is always at liberty to find the precise mathematical function of the invisible curve passing through a succession of randomly scattered points. This is why every action can be said to be insignificant, and every will derisory: incapable of producing a series of actions that is in any way different from one produced by pure chance.

Like all drunks, the Consul notices a constant wavering in the markers of time and space. His life lives itself out in an "uncertain" time and space: "incerto tempore incertisque locis," as Lucretius says of the declination of atoms and their unpredictable movements. "Had the Station Master said the third or fourth train from which way? Which was North, West? And, anyhow, whose north, whose west? . . . Was it tomorrow he was supposed to meet the train? What had the Station Master said?" (pp. 282–83). This constant interference within his coordinates does not prevent the Consul from standing firm, from facing up to the malicious movement of his surroundings: "Oozing alcohol from every pore, the Consul stood at the open door of the Salon Ofelia. How sensible to have had a mescal! How sensible!" (p. 284).

We would be wrong, however, to think that the Consul has simply lost his sense of direction. That would be the case for an ordinary drunk, for one whose existential framework might vacillate only during his "bouts" and then fall back into place once the crisis was past. But Malcolm Lowry's Consul is no ordinary drunk. He is an extraordinary drunk, a visionary who knows he is submerged in a state of exceptional intoxication. He is not at all like the man who loses his way from time to time, only to find it again and then lose it again. The Consul's drunkenness is permanent, and his resulting state of clairvoyance is subject to no eclipse. No interval of "lucidity" ever troubles his stupor. There no longer exist for him any paths to lose or any paths to find: there are not now and never have been any true paths. The Consul has not lost his sense of direction; it is, rather, the paths themselves that have disappeared everywhere around him—and with them all possibility of a direction. The straight path has been lost in the dark forest, as it was at the beginning of Dante's *Divine Comedy*, of which *Under the Volcano*, by the author's own admission, is a sort of modern, drunken version.

"In the middle of the path of my life I found myself in a dark forest, for the straight path had been lost" (Dante, *Inferno*, I, 1–3). This loss of the straight path has taken place not because such paths are lacking for the Consul but because, on the contrary, they have proliferated. Such paths have enveloped the whole of reality, a reality that is no longer anything other than an infinite intersecting of paths, an impenetrable forest of paths. And if everything is indifferently a path, nothing is a path. There is no direction that does not become confused with every other direction, just as, for Heraclitus, the path that mounts becomes confused with the path that descends. And there is nothing that is not a path, nothing that is not a determined direction. To realize this, it is enough to try to walk aimlessly—an impossible task if ever there was one. We might well, it is true, move around without any determined intention, or stagger along like a drunkard. But in the final analysis, the itinerary we have followed will still have all the signs of determination. It is impossible, in the strict sense of the word, to walk aimlessly, just as it is impossible, in a more general way, to do anything that does not possess the determination of something. You can do whatever you wish, but you can never, for all that, do "anything at all." The manifestations of chance occur only insofar as they are also manifestations of what is determined—that is, of necessity itself.

It is for this reason that Lucretius's *incertum* is always at the same time something determined, a *certum*. And conversely, the signs of what is determined are always at the same time signs of what is undetermined, of chance. Since the necessary condition of all things is that, insofar as they exist, they be determined, it follows that there is nothing that just happens that is not also determined and, for the same reason, nothing determined that does not also just happen. And that is why Lowry says of the Consul and Yvonne that "somehow, anyhow, they moved on."

This passing observation about the Consul's manner is only apparently insignificant. Upon reflection, we discover in it a profound paradox that concerns not only the way a man walks, whether or not he be drunk, but the fate of all things in the world. What is this paradox? It turns, here, on the merging of an idea with its exact opposite: the fact that the "any way at all" coincides perfectly with "not at all any way, but in exactly this way." There is no "anyhow" that does not lead to a "somehow," to something that is not at all anything, anyhow, but, on the contrary, is this reality and no other, this way of being and no other. Total indetermination and total determination are forever equivalent to each other. No element of chance will protect the aleatory from the necessity that it come to exist as this particular thing and as nothing other than this. What is certain, certain anyhow, is that all indetermination ceases at the threshold of existence—that is, that nothing will ever truly be "anyhow" because there is no "anyhow" that is not, as soon as it exists, a *somehow*.

We shall call the "insignificance of the real" this property, inherent to all reality, that it always be simultaneously accidental and determined, both anyhow and somehow. What tips all reality over into nonsense is precisely the necessity it is under to be *always* significant. There is no road that does not have a direction (its own), no construct that does not have a structure (its own), nothing in the world that, even if it delivers no legible message, is not precisely determined and determinable.

The principles of this general insignificance can be summed up in two simple formulas:

1. Every reality is necessarily determined.

This is evident by virtue of the principle of identity $(A = A)$, which is not a truism of no interest but can in many cases become violent and unacceptable.

2. Every reality is necessarily something or other (*quelconque*).

In fact, the necessity of determination is simultaneously a sign of the fortuitous. Determination is not necessary because a thing is this and not that, nor because it is this or that, but because it cannot escape the necessity of being something, or being something or other. Thus, since all reality is equally and necessarily determined, it is also equally and necessarily something or other.

The site of insignificance, the place where all paths coexist and merge, can obviously not be described as a state, because it is the negation of all states. Yet it can, at the same time, be described as a state par excellence. It possesses, in fact, that very virtue missing from the most tenacious stabilities and the most durable constructs—that of *being unsusceptible to any modification*. Here we have a total assurance about the future: nothing will ever happen that will contradict the principle of insignificance; whatever happens will always be something, something both determined and something or other. All future paths belong already to the present confusion of paths. There is, in fact, an insurmountable contradiction between the notions of chance and of modification. If what exists is essentially chance (*hasard*), it follows that what exists cannot be modified by any undetermined element (*aléa*), by any "event"—in that no event, in the sense of something erupting within yet distinct from the field of chance, can ever occur. Changing in an unforeseeable way, the real only confirms itself in its state: it has not changed. Chance will never be changed by chance. This is why every event, no matter how agreeable or desirable, becomes derisory when we begin to interpret it as philosophers rather than as historians or politicians. In more philosophical and perhaps more sibylline terms: *something* can modify *something*, but *nothing* cannot modify *nothing*. And the real is nothing—nothing stable, nothing constructed, nothing fixed. Therefore, reality is not, in itself, modifiable.

In a quite similar way, Lucretius proposes a theory of monotony—*"eadum sunt semper omnia"* (*De rerum natura*, III, 945)—that in no way contradicts his theory of perpetual change, but rather confirms and clarifies it. What exists only in changing cannot be modified by the fact that it changes. That everything is always the same means, then, that everything is always equally fortuitous, equally ephemeral, and equally changing. This is the reason for the uniformity of the world according to Lucretius: the world is unable to change its form or its constitution because it is constitutionally without form.

Lowry expresses beautifully this non-modification inherent to every changing state. The Consul, drunk, is seated at a table in the restaurant of the Salon Ofelia with his half-brother and Yvonne as he ponders the condition of his "being-in-the-world": "The Consul sat, fully dressed however, not moving a muscle. Why was he here? Why was he always more or less, here?" (p. 294). He can move about all he wants, go where he likes, but he knows he will always find himself, with only insignificant variations, in the same place, at the same point. The Consul is approaching a great ontological revelation: the truth that being able to exist anywhere at all does not dispense him from the necessity of existing, each time, somewhere. Always somewhere, always here then, more or less. Always, by all ways: whatever be the path. . . .

The insignificance of the real is not limited to those cases where reality presents itself in an obviously incoherent and disorderly way, in a state of pure and arbitrary contiguity. It appears even more clearly when the real manifests itself as coherent, orderly, and continuous, forming a text that may be more or less elaborate, more or less rudimentary. In this sense, the real is like a bad writer: although he may finally have little to say, he is more than happy to write about it. And silence, if it is the last word reality has to offer us, is never so eloquent as when the real speaks. This disguised silence, this silence clothed in speech, is far more revealing than pure silence. In the same way, chance (*le hasard*) is never more impressive than when it takes on the appearance of purpose. It is for this reason that Aristotle insists on the distinction between the simply fortuitous (*automaton*) and true chance (*tychē*), in which what is purely fortuitous disguises itself as an apparent purposefulness.

There are innumerable "texts" in the world—harbingers of a meaning that never arrives, bearers of an empty message—that offer us such insignificant significance. In the physical world, it is enough that there be some manifestation of regularity for us to see that regularity as a text, a message, and a temptation to infer significance. Consider the example of the eclipses of the moon and sun. We know that solar eclipses, despite slight variation, occur in a very regular manner throughout periods, called *Saros*, of 18 years and 10 or 11 days, at the end of which there begin similar cycles of eclipses that will occur on approximately the same days and in the same order. Given the complexity and precariousness of the conditions required for an eclipse, this regularity in their appearance seems nothing short of a miracle. In effect, for an eclipse to occur, the following principal conditions must be met:

1. There must be an alignment Sun-Earth-Moon (or Sun-Moon-Earth), that is, a period of a full or a new moon, determined by the synodic revolution or *lunar month*, "S," where

$$S = 29.530588 \text{ days}$$

2. The sun must pass in proximity to the "nodes" (i.e., the two points where the lunar orbit passes through the ecliptic), as determined by the *eclipse year*, "E" (whose length is different from that of a normal year because the nodes regress on the ecliptic), where:

$$E = 346.6200 \text{ days}$$

3. The moon must pass through the same nodes, as happens during each *draconic month*, "D," where:

$$D = 27.2122 \text{ days}$$

4. Finally, there must be a compensation for the irregularities in the apparent movement of the bodies involved, especially the irregularity of the moon in its rather pronounced elliptical motion. The principal lunar irregularity is a function of its distance at the

perigee of its orbit, or its anomaly. Thus an *anomalistic month*, "A," is defined as the interval between two passages of the moon at the perigee:

$$A = 27.5546 \text{ days}$$

Given these conditions, a pattern in the appearances of the eclipses becomes imaginable only if, by some chance, there exists a common multiple of the values S, E, D, and A. The smaller this common multiple, the greater will be the regularity of eclipses, and the shorter the period before the cycle begins again.

As a matter of fact, such a common multiple does exist, and it is surprisingly small: the figure 6,585. In effect:

1. $223 \times 29.530588 = 6,585.3211$
2. $19 \times 346.6200 \quad = 6,585.78$
3. $242 \times 27.2122 \quad = 6,585.3524$
4. $239 \times 27.5546 \quad = 6,585.5494$

In other words, thanks to these happy arithmetical coincidences, the period of 6,585 days covers approximately 223 lunar months, 19 eclipse years, 242 draconic months, and 239 anomalistic months. This is the *Saros* period, which spans 18 years plus either 10 or 11 days, depending on whether the 18-year interval includes four or five leap years.

No example more elegantly expresses the relation between chance and regularity, nor confirms more convincingly Lucretius's thesis that order is nothing other than a particular case of disorder. What we have here is a case of chance events producing a regularity that in no way attests to an order within nature, but only to an accident in the normal course of things, an accident produced by chance. In terms of this particular example, we must distinguish between two levels of chance: an element of physical chance concerning the world, and an element of mathematical chance independent of what happens in the sky. The element of physical chance lies in the fact that a number of movements occur in periods whose arithmetic correspondences are the figures 223,19,242, and 239, respectively. The element of mathematical chance lies in the fact that 223, 19, 242, and 239 are all common denominators of 6,585. There is, properly speaking, no such thing as arithmetic necessity. What necessity is there, for example, to the distribution of prime numbers (i.e., whole numbers divisible only by themselves or by unity), or to the series of natural numbers (the series of wholes)? Why is there a prime number in the fifth, seventh, and eleventh positions? It is a purely accidental distribution; yet these prime numbers generate all possible numerical series. The same accidental distribution occurs in the sequence of numbers following the decimal point in π; yet this series of apparently chance figures nonetheless expresses the invariant and necessary rapport between the circle and its diameter. Even at the heart of pure mathematics, that science most independent of any compromise with things, we again find the Janus face of all reality: as one face proclaims necessity, the other always proclaims chance.

"How surprising that there be so little mystery to the eclipses!" proclaims the Marquise on the second evening of Fontenelle's *Entretiens sur la pluralité des mondes habités.* Nothing could be less mysterious, in effect; and nothing simpler. It is so simple, in fact, that there is nothing to understand: the phenomenon of eclipses occurs without reason—if by reason we mean a necessary arrangement of things. That, however, is certainly not the way in which Fontenelle wished the Marquise's reply to be taken. He must, rather, have thought: it is simple because it is natural (no need to invoke hidden or supernatural causes), and it proves that there is order in the world.

Today we would tend to think, and rightly so, that it is very complex and that it proves nothing. What, in fact, have we learned about the world by observing the regularity of eclipses? Nothing; except perhaps that a series of events we would expect to occur in complete disorder occurs, for no particular reason, in a very regular way. We might well learn just as much if we took to counting our farts in order to establish some sort of statistics. Beckett suggests this in *Molloy*: "One day I counted them. Three hundred and fifteen farts in nineteen hours, or an average of over sixteen farts an hour. After all, it's not excessive. Four farts every fifteen minutes. It's nothing. Not even one fart every four minutes. It's unbelievable. Damn it, I hardly fart at all, I should never have mentioned it. Extraordinary how mathematics help you to know yourself."[10]

"Without noticing it, biochemistry falls into the invincible illusion that, since it has carried out a measurement, it has in fact measured something."[11] In the same way, after asking so many questions, we gen-

---

[10] Samuel Beckett, *Molloy* (New York, 1955), p. 30.
[11] François Dagognet, *Philosophie biologique* (Paris, 1955), p. 82.

erally end up imagining that we hear answers. This touches on the great problem of "voices" speaking amidst the silence—voices that have never had trouble finding listeners, even such distinguished listeners as Joan of Arc and André Malraux. In the same way, after so much reading, we generally imagine we are reading a message . . . .

The examples cited thus far—the aimless wandering of Lowry's Consul, the occurrence of eclipses—testify, on different levels, to the same silence of the real, the same *monotony*: that of a real that speaks, but that emits only one sound (*monos tonos*) and conveys only one meaning, like the straight curves mathematicians produce from what they call "monotonous functions." Only one monotonous meaning: to always have, necessarily, some meaning or other. Meaning never escapes the monotony of being something or other, necessarily not necessary. The messages coming to us from the real are always finally indifferent because they carry the same monotonous and insignificant content. "The secret of things is that there is no secret. Their profound message is only noise, none makes a sign to me, and there is no signal . . . that there be nothing to read at the end of every reading, who can tolerate it?"[12]

Curiously—and contrary to what we might spontaneously expect—philosophy has a tendency not to refuse but to solicit imaginary meanings. It is here that wonder and admiration, cited by Plato in the

[12] Michel Serres, *Hermes III: La Traduction* (Paris, 1974), p. 67.

Theaetetus as the philosophical virtues par excellence, take on particularly ambiguous overtones. For if the philosopher might justifiably be surprised that things exist (that there be being), he should not be surprised that things be such as they are, ferreting out in their particular arrangement some hidden meaning that is as tautological as it is obscure. If things are such as they are, it cannot be by chance, decides a certain form of philosophical reason—whereas true reason would lead us to think that if things are what they are, it is because they cannot escape the necessity of being something or other.

Hegel is the great philosopher of imaginary meaning: thinking that all the real is rational, that nothing happens by chance, that everything that happens is the sign of a secret destiny that it is up to the philosopher to understand and unveil. Quite in opposition to the pointless unfolding of history, the Hegelian philosopher reads the hidden meaning and necessity of all that seems, but only seems, to occur without purpose and without reason. All reality is doubled by an imaginary meaning. Hegel accepts the real only insofar as it signifies. It was for this reason that he scorned mathematics since, well before Russell, he knew that it constituted a clear and precise language, but one that speaks of nothing and transmits no message. The real real, for the Hegelian philosopher, is cut from another cloth. On October 13, 1806, for example, Hegel caught a glimpse of Napoleon riding through the streets of Jena. The man he saw was not a chief of state seated on his horse and looking over the town he had just taken, but rather the "world spirit" whose presence on that day, at that hour, in that place, seemed a kind of wonder: "I saw the emperor, that world spirit, cross the streets of the town on horseback. It is an incredible feeling to see such an individual who, concentrated in one point, seated on his horse, nonetheless extends over the entire world."[13]

It seems that Hegel could not grasp the necessity that every man, whatever his historical importance, must exist, at every moment, in one place or another. No: Napoleon's presence, *hic et nunc*, is a miracle. Were he in another place at another time, his existence would still be a miracle. It is a case not so much of idolatry for a great man as of a superstition with regard to history as something meaningful. If history harbors any meaning, it effectively reveals itself here; it appears for an instant at this point in space where the emperor is "concentrated." Given that, we can understand Hegel's fascination with being a few steps from the great secret. What impresses Hegel about Napoleon is not the man, not the emperor of the French, but the bearer of history. It is not a man, as great as he may be, who crosses the streets of Jena— it is History that passes by and for a moment becomes visible to the eyes of the young Hegel in the person of Napoleon. It is a history, however, whose precise meaning cannot immediately be defined, for the trick of history, and the trick of meaning, is that those most touched by it live it and create it without being able to penetrate its meaning. The course of things may ap-

13 R. Rosenkranz, *Hegels Leben* (Berlin, 1844), p. 229.

pear insignificant, but these things must manifest the unfolding of a meaning. Apparently nothing of importance is happening, but in reality, *something is happening*. What exactly? That you will know later, when Minerva's bird has definitively taken flight.

We might well insist here on the innumerable moral, religious, and political effects of this madness—this madness for meaning that is madness par excellence, a madness for which there is no philosophical antidote other than the intransigent materialism of a Lucretius or an Epicurus (and not that of a Marx). The taking seriously of what is precisely not serious (the insignificant becomes the essential, reading the paper becomes the "morning prayer"); the compliant perception of importance where there is nothing of importance; the religious and docile state of mind ready to recognize in every pompous blowhard a messenger of History, if not a messenger of God; the ideas of good and evil (depending on whether one favors or resists this particular advent of meaning); the obsession with participating in the advent of meaning and all its ensuing dangers; the inevitability of intolerance and persecution—these are only a few, among many others, of that madness's more unpleasant effects.

This obstinate quest for meaning is in itself little more than an unfortunate mental proclivity. It becomes truly disturbing only when, suddenly claiming to have "discovered" the sought-after meaning, it succeeds. This search for meaning is like an endemic illness whose fits correspond to moments of inspiration, to those moments when we think we have found meaning. The philosophers and literati of the nineteenth century provide excellent examples of such fits. They were constantly seized by the fever of discovering the great secret of all things—and generally they found what they were looking for. In their eyes, the elements of the real were like the scattered pages of a great book that had been mislaid or had not yet been found, even though it was so clearly within reach. In isolation, these events mean nothing. They will yield their meaning only if we are able to find the book, for then we shall read the meaning of each "passage" of the real as a function of its place in the great book of the world. Every aspect of the real is welcomed like a new fragment of that long-sought overall meaning, like a new piece of the puzzle that must sooner or later be completed.

This explains the great number of works heralding the revelation of the general meaning of all things within some heteroclite synthesis elaborating correspondences between the most disparate elements, mixing the most dissimilar questions and levels, and generally allowing itself the most reckless use of recent scientific discoveries, particularly those touching the areas of gravitation, magnetism, and electricity. One of these strange syntheses can be found in a seldom-read work by Edgar Allen Poe, *Eureka.* "Eureka," that is, "I have found." "I have found the secret of the universe," declared Poe to his publisher, G. P. Putnam, as he brought him the manuscript. But a reading of *Eureka* does not in the least fulfill the expectations created in the mind of the reader. For the most part, it consists of references to the principles of gravitation, attraction (entropy), and repulsion (differentiation) as well as vague thoughts about what Baudelaire, who later translated *Eureka*, would call the "mysterious and profound unity" of all things. Having read the book, we ask ourselves in vain what Poe actually discovered. I have found; so be it—but found *what*?

The most remarkable thing about this particular *Eureka* is that, although exactly nothing has been discovered, the author is convinced he has made a tremendous discovery and is revealing to his readers a fabulous secret. It is not as though *Eureka* offered some false theory, some fantastical doctrine, or some visionary hypothesis. There is no theory at all, and the book has precisely nothing to say. This peculiarity of imagining that one has found something, yet being incapable of saying what that something is, is not unique to Poe. In fact, his position is only apparently peculiar. Upon reflection, we realize that this happens every time we attempt to make some revelation about the overall meaning of the real. Since there is in fact nothing to say about that subject, the person who sincerely believes he has something to say is quite logically forced to say nothing. In such cases, it is a question of a feeling, a feeling that is purely formal and not about to be troubled by any specific content or object. The feeling is that there is a meaning, that there is a secret to be revealed, and even that I have revealed that secret. Such a feeling has no need of precision and actually does much better without it. This is why Poe can sincerely believe that he is revealing the secret of the universe to the readers of *Eureka* while at the same time he forgets to specify what key and what secret he is talking about. Predictably, revealing such a secret obeys a structure analogous to that of all belief: a structure characterized by the simple fact of believing, and independent of any particular content. Believing need not imply that one believes in something. On the contrary, the presence of any direct object for the verb *to believe* should be avoided at all costs. The conviction that there is meaning becomes, for Poe as for anyone else, all the stronger to the extent that he is unsure, not that there is meaning, but of what that meaning might be.

I have claimed that all reality is necessarily something or other (*quelconque*), that it is both determined and fortuitous, and therefore insignificant. I have also claimed that when we attribute a meaning to the real, we are giving it an imaginary value, a value that is added to the perception of a reality that can itself always be interpreted in terms of simple chance. I have further claimed that there is no secret of History and no mystery of becoming. Becoming is without mystery because it happens like the aimless wandering of Lowry's Consul, *somehow, anyhow*: anyhow, somehow; that is, in any way at all. It is strange that so much intellectual energy should be wasted on trying to uncover the meaning of becoming and the reason of History: the meaning of that which has no meaning.

These statements, and the general thesis they express, are not meant as descriptive but as critical propositions. Their intent is not to describe, and even less to exhaust, the richness of the real. They are meant instead to call into question other judgments of the real, judgments made in terms of meanings or values that are like so many shadows cast on the true "value" or "nature" of the real. Surrendering the real to insignificance means surrendering the real to itself, dispelling its false meanings. This surrender is not meant to imply that reality is absurd or uninteresting. Above all, it is not intended to depict the existence of reality as trivial, and thus to ignore or facilely elide the ontological question. I have said that what exists is meaningless and that chance can adequately explain all that exists. This thesis remains ambiguous if we fail to specify that it focuses on what happens *in* existence, but not at all on *the fact* of existence itself, the fact that something exists. Of this particular fact—that there is something and not nothing—it is pointless to claim that it is either "meaningful" or "meaningless." It is pointless to try to think anything about it at all, unless you are a visionary or in contact with God as the author of ontological fact. In the same way, chance (*le hasard*), which allows us to understand calmly all the pure hazards (*les aléas*) of existence, in no way helps us to understand the fact of existence itself: to say that being exists by chance would be absurd. There is no mystery in things, but there is a mystery *of* things. It is pointless to scrutinize and try to extract from them a secret that does not exist.

It is at their surface, on the edge of their existence, that they are incomprehensible: not because they are such and such, but simply because they are.

A rapid examination of the major themes and theses of modern philosophy, especially the most recent, immediately reveals the persistence and permanence of the question of meaning. This question is always part of the agenda and always current, because the search for and affirmation of meaning seem to be among those things that never change and that most probably can never change. There are, in fact, good reasons for thinking that the question of meaning is such that it cannot fail to be asked and continually re-asked—and this despite whatever one might think of the question's lack of seriousness or relevance.

To be permanent—to continue no matter what happens—an investigation must satisfy a twofold condition: it must be founded on a desire that will never abate, and it must be incapable of succeeding. The will to find must be unshakable and the risk of discovery nonexistent: only then will the investigation be forever open. Imagine, for example, a criminal investigation, driven by the most powerful forces, which is attempting at all costs to discover the identity of an assassin who does not exist. That file will never find its way to Cases Closed.

What today are the most frequent and noteworthy forms of this search for meaning? One might, in response to this question, identify a major trend that has established itself under the tutelage of the illusionist.

Philosophical illusionism consists of proclaiming a meaning without ever showing it, just as an illusionist uses his powers of suggestion to convince his audience that they see an object that is absent. Hegel might well be invoked as the father of this illusionism. He is the philosopher who discovers in each thing the manifestation of Reason, of Idea, and of Spirit, but who never clarifies the nature of this Idea, this Spirit, or this Reason. There is no doubt that Hegel, his every page bristling with philosophical genius, develops with extraordinary speculative power the circumstances, moments, mediations, tricks, false appearances, and misleadingly incomplete perspectives through which meaning comes to be as becoming unfolds. But this teaches us nothing about the nature of meaning itself, unless we agree with Hegel that the notions of Idea, Reason, and Spirit are so clear that they need no definition or explication. That perhaps is the privilege of "Absolute Knowledge": to dispense with all particular knowledge and to dispense with having to specify what it is we know.

The modern Hegelians, from Stéphane Mallarmé to Jacques Lacan, Georges Bataille, and Jacques Derrida, make use of the same philosophical illusionism, but with one difference: meaning is no longer announced as present but as still to come, as something interminably deferred. The invisibility of meaning— of a meaning thought of as visible by Hegel and his immediate disciples—is henceforth accepted as such, as invisible. It is a provisional invisibility, the awaiting of a visibility that is still and perhaps forever to come. But for the time being, the "work of the concept" is not finished; in fact, we are still a long way short of that. With Hegel we had to be patient, we had to wait for a real grasp of the concept as we progressed through a laborious and interminable series of mediations. But finally these mediations did succeed and converged on the emergence of a meaning, *hic et nunc*, and on a "reconciliation" with the present.

For the modern Hegelians, however, mediation never succeeds. Still and forever mediating, each mediation differs from what it is finally meant to mediate, that is, from what Hegel would call the "thing itself." In this respect, each mediation constitutes both a "difference" in the Hegelian sense and a *"différance"* in the Derridean sense of something that is forever deferred. It is a question, one might say, of an unhappy Hegelianism: unhappy because it leads nowhere, but an Hegelianism all the same. Examining it more closely, we might say that this is an immoderate and unreserved Hegelianism. It is immoderate because the role of negativity is no longer, as it was for Hegel, in any way moderated. Now freed from its service to any ultimately positive outcome, negativity operates only for itself, without limit or moderation. It is without reserve because there is now no limit to how long we might postpone the interruption of the dialectic process by some final term, by a final *Aufhebung*. This is an endless Hegelianism, a Hegelianism without "eschatology": an infinite Hegelianism, like the *Entretien* of the same name by Mau-

rice Blanchot.[14] Derrida's unhappy Hegelianism, for
example, diagnoses in this incompletion of the dialectic the echo of an originary "lack," an "originary
non-presence" that he calls "*différance*" as a "process
of deferring which both splits and delays presence."[15]
Although we might think we are tolling the bell (*son-
ner le Glas*) for Hegel, we are in fact still at matins.

This movement brings with it a change and a re-
finement in the way the illusionism of meaning is
practiced. It is no longer a question of suggesting the
presence of a meaning through the "near sorcery" that
Koyré attributed to Hegel, but of exhibiting a nothing,
of drawing the spectator's attention to something that
is not only invisible but that everyone acknowledges
to be invisible—and this while reserving the right to
suggest, because of that very absence of meaning, the
presence of a meaning *elsewhere*. Of course you *see*
that meaning is elsewhere, since you *see* that it is not
here. This is a sophisticated illusionism that no
longer need exploit the crude powers of suggestion.
Among the first practitioners of this disappointed but
persistent Hegelianism were Mallarmé and, in the
twentieth century, Bataille. Bataille's work—a description of eroticism as the experience of an impossible moving beyond (*dépassement*), of a series of mediations that are vainly and indefinitely transgressed
one after the other in the hope of reaching that thing
itself which is never accessible—is a remarkable illustration of both Hegelian nostalgia and the illusionism of meaning.

[14] Maurice Blanchot, *L'Entretien infini* (Paris, 1969).
[15] Jacques Derrida, *La Voix et le phénomène* (Paris, 1967), p. 98.

We set out to follow meaning: in the sense, for example, that one "follows" the seminar of Lacan—not with the hope of some revelation, but out of fascination with a master whose penetration and omniscience are measured in direct proportion to his litotes and his silences. More than anyone else of recent memory, Lacan knew how to fascinate. By the display of a nothing, an empty place, a silence, he led his audience (and his readers) to experience nothingness and emptiness in an almost material way as something, as the hollow inside of a full outside, as the silence of a word that is elsewhere eloquent and that might explain everything if only it could be heard. This silent word becomes the veiled sign of a meaning, a meaning that Lacan knows but that he must never allow himself to divulge. The signifier is a hieroglyphic: at once implausible because it says nothing, yet plausible because it brings meaning from Elsewhere.

Lacan does proclaim a meaning, and if you do not understand it, it is because that meaning is elsewhere. He does show you the object, and if you see nothing, it is because it is missing from its place. He does designate the Other, and if you see no one, it is precisely because it is the other, and not the one you are looking at. His Hegelian reading of the principal Freudian concepts ends up making the phallus, castration, and the murder of the father so many "moments" during which the thing means by its very absence. This modern avatar of Hegelianism—a passage from the presence of meaning within the concrete to a relegation of meaning to an elsewhere, to an absence—was already at the heart of Mallarmé's poetic enterprise, and it is Mallarmé's style that Lacan set out to rediscover and renew. For Mallarmé, as for Lacan, meaning is real but absent, exactly like the poetic flower, that "absent of all bouquets."

There is also a certain kinship between Lacan's notion of the Signifier and Kafka's notion of the Law. Both are presented as something infinitely close at hand yet always deferred, always put off until the morrow. The faithful student at Lacan's seminar was surprisingly like the man in the famous parable from *The Trial* who waits to be admitted to the Law:

Before the Law stands a doorkeeper. To this doorkeeper there comes a man who begs for admittance to the Law. But the doorkeeper says that he cannot admit the man at the moment. The man, on reflection, asks if he will be allowed, then, to enter later. "It is possible," answers the doorkeeper, "but not at this moment." . . . The doorkeeper gives him a stool and lets him sit down at the side of the door. There he sits waiting for days and years.[16]

Even the ending of this parable seems to evoke Lacan. We remember that the man, now grown old and about to die, asks the doorkeeper the simple favor of answering one question: How can it be that he is the only one to be waiting in front of the door of the Law? Because this door was only for you, answers the doorkeeper. Now I am leaving and I am closing the door. It is the same with Lacan: this meaning you seek in

[16] Franz Kafka, *The Trial* (New York, 1969), pp. 267–68.

vain, which I know but will not tell you, which you will never know—rest assured that it does exist, that I do know it, and that it really is *exactly* the meaning you have been looking for. We are not even left with the modest hope that what we are looking for but can never find might just be nothing.

Reading, Criticism, Theory

On Reading Again

François Roustang

Reading occupies much of a professor of literature's time, yet this daily exercise remains deeply mysterious because of its extreme complexity. Following the example of many others, who have perhaps provided better answers, I too would like once again to ask myself the question: What is reading? As my title suggests, I would like to pose this question in a more precise form: What happens when we reread a text? For although I may read a text only once without ever returning to it, I have never been able to study a work without engaging in numerous rereadings. When I read a text only once, whether it fall within the province of philosophy, of literature, or of the essay, it remains inaccessible to me; I don't understand it. I don't understand what it wants to tell me; I don't understand how it is constructed. I don't understand how it differs from other writings of the same kind.

I had this experience yet again when I began reading Casanova. At first *The Story of My Life* (*Memoirs*) seemed to me merely a series of more or less curious anecdotes, apparently little related to one another.

Since I had nevertheless been struck by the oddness of some of them, I began rereading these passages once or a number of times. I remained puzzled until I was struck by the repetition of certain leitmotifs. Undoubtedly, if this repetition did not reveal the outlines of a structure, it at least reflected the steadfastness of a preoccupation. But only after additional readings did I become aware of the shifts between corresponding components as I passed from one episode to another. A nosebleed in one story, for example, became a defloration in another and an attack of apoplexy in yet a third. Or, again, in one story magic gave way to religious belief, while in another it took on the overtones of a blasphemous act. In order for these transformations and the principle behind them to become absolutely clear, I had to familiarize myself with the text in all its permutations. What I mean by this is that I had to be able to recall all its elements, whether my reading began at the beginning, in the middle, or at the end, because episodes like the ones mentioned above do not follow the same sequence within each story.

From these remarks I would deduce my first principle of rereading: *one must reread until the text can be broken down into its basic components*. This activity cannot be compared to the work involved in making a jigsaw puzzle. In the puzzle, the image is cut up according to laws that are not its own. I would imagine that when puzzles are manufactured industrially, the same cutting mold is used time and again regardless of the nature of the images, drawings, and landscapes offered to challenge the buyer's patience.

The effect of rereading a text cannot be imagined in this way. If it could, it would be equivalent to photocopying a literary text and tearing the copy into pieces according to the impulses of a momentary irritation. We would then have reduced the text to its components. Reading, on the contrary, involves keeping the entire text in one's memory so that each and every one of its features can intercommunicate. This results in a feeling of haphazard multiplicity that cannot help but discourage us initially. But from this very discouragement the light will be born.

I would like to focus upon a decisive moment in reading, which often remains unnoticed and about which we very rarely speak: the moment when we feel we have been overcome by the immeasurable complexity of the text. It is piecemeal in our memory, and we are convinced we shall never be able to make anything of it, that it has overwhelmed us, and that our work as critics must come to a halt. During my study of Casanova (though I could say the same of many other readings), not once, after an extended rereading of one or many chapters, was I able to avoid the depressing feeling that I had better abandon my work, that those anecdotes were certainly meaningless and unconnected, that my previous hypotheses or my little discoveries were no longer confirmed, and that I had best abandon all hope of continuing. In fact, however, my passage through this moment of discouragement and impotence led to dawning light. Most often this happened at night or on awakening. In that mixture of confusion and extreme lucidity, an idea would surface, or a group of ideas would reorganize the whole of the text and enable me to see the structure I was looking for. If we so often have only a meager understanding of the texts we read, it is because we are afraid of encountering the difficult moment during which all our research seems to fade away. This moment of darkness, this passage through incomprehension, cannot be feigned. It must be real, and the text must truly have made us lose our footing and our feeling of mastery over it. There is no understanding that is not born of incomprehension, no understanding that is, which is somewhat creative.

The relationships that then appear involve, as do all relationships, links and breaks. Certain passages move closer to others in a completely unexpected way, while others separate from each other in spite of the fact that up until then they were juxtaposed. To arrive at this point, however, it is necessary to respect the whole of the text, to take into account all its components, even, if possible, down to its smallest details. I would therefore formulate my second principle of rereading as: *a text has been respected only when we have taken its totality into account*. This, it seems to me, is an imperative sometimes overlooked in criticism. It can happen that brilliant interpretations are given of a literary work, but the reader quickly realizes that the critic was satisfied with gathering from here and there in the text only those elements that justify a pre-established thesis or world view. Using this method, it is undoubtedly possible to pass in review the whole of literature and to demonstrate that it confirms the idea one started with—for

truly great authors, at least, are sufficiently rich to
have said something about almost everything.

Respecting the whole of a text is much closer to always expecting that we will discover we have been too
hasty in the way we have connected or separated certain components. Most of all, it involves not being
satisfied with our separations and connections so
long as the whole of the text does not find a place in
our interpretation or so long as even one element is
neglected at the moment when we establish the overall structure of the work. This sometimes allows us
to discover that certain details, whose meaning escapes us, are in reality of decisive importance. I tried,
for instance, to show this for the expression "dressed
as a woman," which recurs repeatedly in one of the
first chapters of Casanova's *Memoirs*.

In fact, we know that respecting the whole of a
work is an unattainable ideal, but it can certainly
serve as a regulating principle. An ideal is deadly and
taunts us if we do not achieve it. A regulating principle, however, can guide us without being entirely
achieved. To move toward the whole of the text, our
reading should be endless, for we must move from the
chapter to the paragraph, then from the paragraph to
the sentence, and from the sentence to each of its
parts. This is the way we ought to proceed. I did not
very often take the time while reading Casanova to go
into the analysis of sentences or into the analysis of a
sequence of sentences. Whenever I did, however, I was
reassured because I discovered that his stylistic devices are always in keeping with the workings of the

text as a whole. Great writers reveal their particular style in all the details of their work. It is enough to make the effort to demonstrate this.

We now have at our disposal two apparently contradictory principles for reading: one aims to tear the text to pieces and the other to respect the text as a whole. Let us return now to the effects of the rereading or the continued reading of a text—one might say, of inhabiting it.

Have you ever happened to look at one object for a long time, a very long time, be it the leaf of a tree or a great painting? After a certain period the object in question disintegrates. It loses its global character and reveals pieces and structures that were not at all apparent when you first looked at it. If you were to stare even longer, you might end up asking whether you were not the victim of a hallucination. It is as though we ourselves, in a certain sense, become the support of this object, as though we were capable of re-creating it.

I recall a book that made a great impression on me in my childhood. It told the story of a knight who had contemplated a mountain for so long a time that he became the mountain. A persistent rereading seems to me to be a similar experience. In a certain way, the reader becomes the text, he loses himself within it to the point of feeling, of being moved, of thinking and judging like the text, which imposes itself on him.

But, as I have just noted, one can also observe an opposite phenomenon, which occasionally takes place in scientific research. A biologist who, over a period of years, has observed a certain type of cell arrives at a point where he no longer knows whether what he sees is actually the object he is describing or if his own brain and eye invent the object. The same thing happens when we have spent so much time with a text that we ask ourselves if we are still reading or if we are not reconstituting it in our own way.

Thus repeated readings of a text produce a double effect: either we lose ourselves in the text, or we lose the text in favor of our own prejudices and obsessions. The third principle of rereading can therefore be expressed as follows: *rereading involves a certain violence on the part of both text and reader*. If I read as a critic, it is so that the text will provide me with an explanation of itself, of its content, its structure, and its form. This is what understanding a text means, in the same way that one understands a leaf by examining it against the light and discovering how it functions, develops, and dies. In much the same way, one understands the human body today by submitting it to the investigations of modern medicine, which divide it into its component parts and photograph it from all angles and at all depths.

Yet why this violence? It is a response to the text's own violence as an artifact that presents itself to the reader to seduce and capture him, yet at the same time escapes from him in order to preserve the secret of its origin. I am thinking in particular of Diderot's great art in weaving a very subtle canvas in order to prevent the reader from escaping it and yet endlessly leading the reader astray in directions Diderot starts but does not pursue. This becomes caricatural in *Jacques le fataliste*, but one could say the same of Diderot's other novels and—who knows—even of his work as an encyclopedist.

The author is duty bound to misguide the reader. Otherwise he could no longer write. Were the author to be aware of the reader during the writing, the reader's limited understanding of the text would trap the author and prevent him from inventing beyond the possibilities of this always limited readerly comprehension. The same is true of Casanova. The most impressive trick he plays on us is to have us believe he was not a writer but only a casual teller of tales. He also misleads his readers by making them believe that his subjects are purely erotic and that he repeats himself just as tediously as any other author of this kind of literature. I believe I have shown in *The Quadrille of Gender*[1] the subtlety of construction and the extraordinary intellectual acuteness of Casanova's descriptions of the workings of human relations.

I do not wish to enter into a discussion of Casanova here, but only to emphasize that, like all great writers, he misleads his reader in order to blur the contours, both for himself and for the reader, of what he knows without wanting to know it. The critic, paid for knowing or for trying to know, inevitably commits himself to a struggle with the author as to a struggle with someone who tries not to give himself away, but who nevertheless provides all the means necessary for his being discovered, without which there would be no literary work at all.

If the literary text involves a strategy of revealing

[1] François Roustang, *The Quadrille of Gender: Casanova's 'Memoirs'* (Stanford, Calif., 1988).

while concealing, rereading must also invent a strategy, adapted to the text and the author, that seeks to disarm the author in order to unmask him. I have already noted that one of the decisive moments in this struggle is characterized by the fading away of all mastery on the reader's part. It is at the moment when the author has succeeded in creating a doubt in the reader's mind about possibly comprehending the text at all that understanding has a chance of seeing the light of day. When the author has won, when the reader is totally disarmed, then the reader, who had entered the dark night of confusion, can return with all his strength—and then it is the author who has lost the battle.

Thus the link between author and reader, the passage from the first's creation to the latter's understanding, takes place at exactly the moment when both find themselves disarmed and defenseless, lost and deprived of mastery. It is at what I would call this point of horror that they communicate with each other. I shall certainly not be teaching you anything new in saying that one of the characteristics of a great literary work—a work that crosses borders and centuries—is its capacity to make us feel some impenetrable aspect of human suffering, of the paroxysm and fascination of this suffering.

This leads me to the formulation of the fourth principle: *a reading that does not reach the point of horror cannot even begin to understand the text's source.* You will undoubtedly argue that this is hardly obvious in the work of Casanova. I believe I have clearly shown the opposite. Starting with the narration of his first childhood memories, we are already at that point: the shame of mistreatment, his terror in the face of a possessed and hysterical woman, the macabre games with cut-up cadavers, and so forth. If the reader pays attention, he will notice that the happy periods of love and power are followed by others during which the hero of the comedy descends into the most sordid depths of human experience. For Casanova days of splendor and vanity are never far from those of misery and failure.

It seems to me that we have understood nothing about Casanova if we pass over this point of horror. How otherwise, except from that point, can we explain the variety of the complicated strategies he develops in his relations with women, with gambling, and with magic? Everything is done simultaneously to avoid a return to the horror and to maintain his relationship with it. According to his explicit intentions, he does everything necessary to escape from it, but secretly he arranges everything so that horror will soon make its catastrophic reappearance. He would never have had the success he had, he would never have fascinated generations of readers, if he had been only an amiable comedian, an innocent swindler, or a cheerful womanizer. All his exploits were marked with the red-hot iron of the shameful, the sordid, and the repugnant. In reality it is at this point that the text reveals its unity. Nowhere else can we find the real connection between the three components of Casanova's existence: his hesitation about the differences between the sexes, his refusal to work, his fascination with superstitious practices.

If I insisted earlier on our encountering a moment of discouragement and confusion, it is because it is there that the reader rejoins the text at the exact point where, through horror, he tends to destroy himself. But at the same time, thanks to this horror, the reader has arrived at the text's source. The act of reading must itself pass through the deadly suffering in which the author originally found the strength to create. Nothing is closer to artistic creation than the moment of anguish from which the work's production must originate. The reader must endure this same anguish if he is to arrive at the work's real principle.

(I cannot help referring here to the greatest American literary critic I know of, who has perfectly understood and demonstrated that creation is born of anguish. If you think of Harold Bloom's *Agon: Towards a Theory of Revisionism*,[2] you will be forced to acknowledge that the position I am now taking is patently obvious. In particular, his reading of Freud goes far beyond everything else written on the subject, precisely because it sees anguish as being at the very heart of the possibility of literary creation, and especially of poetic creation.)

All of this can of course only serve as a point of departure for understanding a text's strategy. The author is transfixed at this point of horror yet never stops wanting to move outside it. One might even say that the whole of the author's work boils down to the double effort of moving away from this point while remaining as close to it as possible. The aim of every

[2] Harold Bloom, *Agon: Towards a Theory of Revisionism* (New York, 1982).

great work is to distance itself from this unspeakable suffering by speaking of it as precisely as possible. It is a construction that liberates from radical evil because it represents that evil in the universe of words, because it puts it before our eyes. The author takes leave of the unspeakable by speaking of it. He does not abandon it, because his work is its translation, its image, its representation. The work's failure to rid itself of this suffering resides precisely in its success in letting the horror show through.

The whole of Casanova's autobiography could be read as an attempt to propose ever more complex montages so that he can hide from himself the abyss that constantly threatens to open under his feet. But of course each of these montages inexorably re-creates the risk. One of man's points of horror, for example, lies in the loss of his individuality, which at the level of sexuality can be translated as loss of differentiation between the two sexes. Thus, throughout Casanova's life there is no way of deciding whether his aim was to accentuate or to blur that difference.

Undoubtedly, a hurried look, a rapid reading, leaves the impression that the libertine wants to exhibit his virility; but an attentive rereading suggests that this frenzy conceals a fundamental confusion: Is he not like the woman he is seducing? One cannot simply say that Casanova is afraid of women; what he is afraid of is not being able to maintain his difference and thus of being forced to return to a state of indifferentiation. But I think the situation is even more complex. Casanova not only has a fear, he also has a passion for indistinction, a passion for the horror from which he would nevertheless like to turn away. His first love relationships are marked by a complicated staging that allows him to remain unaware of the individuals and the sexes involved. And at the height of his love life he organizes a game for four in which all roles are interchanged. One sees clearly here how the writer wants us to believe there is differentiation through the multiplication of relationships he initiates; yet in making each of these relationships a form of the others, he wants to reproduce undifferentiation, to bring us back to the horror.

Another montage deals with Casanova's social life. The role work plays for each of us is clear. It allows us to avoid anxiety, ultimate questions, the approach of death—everything that makes up the ever-present core of the unspeakable suffering, that of existing. Casanova never worked, apart from one occasion in Paris when he set up a fabric factory, which he quickly led to bankruptcy by transforming it into a harem. He lived off gambling and the gifts more or less explicitly extorted from his benefactors. His life was an alternation between splendor and misery. He was always ready to return to the sordidness of destitution and fraud. He did nothing very effective to protect himself from this cycle because, even at moments of great success, he needed to rub shoulders with the ignominy of failure—often to the point of succumbing to it.

His moral code was based on a studious intertwining of guilt and irresponsibility, innocence and responsibility. He accepted responsibility only for that of which he was not guilty, and accepted guilt only for that for which he was not responsible. All misfortunes arrived by chance; they were not his doing, and he easily consoled himself knowing that human misfortune is far too radical to be seen as anything other than an effect of fate. He revolted against neither laws nor customs because their reform would never have changed the essence of things. Life itself became a game, for playing was all he could do to forget the horror without ever losing sight of it.

Casanova's relations with the higher powers were marked with the same seal. He had no difficulty asserting that he believed in God and respected religion, but he emptied his beliefs of all content; hence in his company we find ourselves face to face with the flagrant hypocrisy of Roman prelates or the abject vulgarity of monks. And if Casanova's practice of magic expressed his pretensions to omnipotence, it nonetheless led either to panicked defeat or to the basest of swindles. He seems to have been attracted to the heights only as long as they led to the depths—yet another way of telling us that the sublime is nothing but the more or less felicitous translation of an agonizing strangeness.

You will undoubtedly object that all of this has to do with Casanova's psychology and has nothing to do with the text, with its literary structure, or with the work's strategy, which are all that we are interested in. I will undertake, however, to show you, both in the work's largest movements and in its smallest details, that horror and the concomitant necessity to state and to conceal it so as to better reveal it serve as the guide and principle of the text's construction. The style is both that of the person who portrays himself and that of the means by which he portrays himself. One could define Casanova's style as a synchronized game involving two hands, with one always knowing how to undo at any given moment what the other is accomplishing. In any single story, the doing and undoing are subtly intertwined without the reader becoming aware of it. During his stay in Rome, for example, Casanova appears to be concerned with his career and to know how to maneuver his way to success. Yet the story of his progress is interrupted from time to time by details that seem to have nothing to do with the main narrative. One soon notices that these at first insignificant details little by little prepare his failure. Two different stories are skillfully intertwined, that of his triumph and that of his ruin.

I could multiply the examples, but this would involve lengthy analyses that are beyond the scope of this study. Let us look at one page where we clearly see this double strategy at work. Casanova is discussing here the prohibition of incest:

As the Duke walked, he spoke to himself, making a number of reflections on what in moral philosophy is referred to as prejudice. There is not a single philosopher who would dare say that the union of a father with his daughter is something horrible by nature; but the prejudice against it is so strong that it would take a completely depraved mind to trample it underfoot. This is the fruit of a respect for the law which a good education has imparted to a tranquil soul and, thus understood, it is no longer a prejudice but a duty.

This duty can also be considered natural in that nature urges us to give those whom we love the same benefits which we ourselves desire. It would seem that what best suits reciprocity in love is an equality in all things: age, circumstance, and character. At first glance one does not find this equality between a father and a daughter. The respect she must feel for the one who gave her life creates an obstacle to the kind of tenderness she must feel for a lover. If the father possesses his daughter by reason of this paternal authority, he is exercising a kind of tyranny that nature must abhor. Our natural love for correct order also determines that our reason find such a union monstrous. There could only be confusion and insubordination for the offspring of such a union. This union in short is abominable in all aspects; but it is no longer such when the two individuals love each other and know nothing of the extranaeous reason which should prevent them from loving each other. Incest, that eternal subject of Greek tragedies, rather than making me cry, makes me laugh; and if I cry at *Phaedra* it is Racine's art which is responsible.[3]

This page could be entitled: from horror to laughter, to better appreciate the horror. Let us look first at how it is constructed. Initially, the author puts in the mouth of his speaker what he himself or any other philosopher of the Enlightenment might think: declaring the union of a father with his daughter to be horrible is the result of prejudice. But since it is the Duke who says this, the reader can easily dismiss the

[3] F. A. Brockhaus, ed., *Casanova* (Paris, 1960) vol. 7, p. 231.

opinion, which spontaneously goes against one's conscience. The horrible remains horrible, and one must have a depraved mind to think otherwise. Prejudice is a duty. Opening a new paragraph, Casanova seems to speak for himself, and he shows that the sexual union of a father and his daughter is an abomination. Then abruptly the argument turns on itself, the monstrosity is erased by love, and incest provokes only laughter.

In a sense, nothing allowed us to foresee this ending, and if one reads rapidly, as certain commentators have done, Casanova might, thanks to this text, pass as an ardent defender of the incest prohibition. But if one looks more closely, one finds Casanova's particular style: what he does with one hand he undoes with the other. He weaves his text with two contradictory threads, which combine the horror of incest and a generalized laughter about the human condition.

Thus you see here the perfect coincidence of content and form. The fundamental ambiguity characterizing Casanova's thought is conveyed in these literary devices, in the way in which his story develops sentence by sentence.

With this in mind, I can generalize and formulate my final principle of rereading: *a text's construction appears most clearly when we have managed to pass from the point of horror to the point of laughter.* Laughter is the minimal distance that the author has led us to travel from what is tragic in the human condition. We know this clearly from the great comedies—the real ones, those of Shakespeare and Molière, which border on the sordid and are just as capable of making us cry as laugh. Although tragedies do not make us laugh, they are certainly capable of exciting us and giving us pleasure through the very beauty they display and the catharsis they produce in us.

So long as our analysis has not led us to bring these two poles together, it is insufficient. We have not yet grasped the construction of the text we are reading. As I noted above, the question with which the critic is faced can be formulated as follows: How has the author managed to liberate himself from horror without abandoning it? In fact, there is no question of abandoning it. An unspeakable suffering clings to the author's body, and he must convey it in its particularity. A great text is one whose sole purpose is to convey this aspect of our destiny, and yet to find something within each of its readers that will touch him because it is universal.

Reading thus becomes an experience of this horror held at a distance by laughter. What another has resolved we seek in turn to resolve through him. Reading is no longer a combat, but rather a complicity with the author; it becomes a catharsis, miming in reverse the process of creation. We readers are incapable of confronting the horror directly because we would not be capable of working it through to the point of laughter. It is better then to rely on somebody else who has given us a tolerable representation of it.

The Gesture of Criticism

Roy Roussel

This is an essay about the way we experience our desire to know a literary
work. Specifically, it is about the way structuralist
and post-structuralist thinking inevitably destroyed
the "innocence" of this initial desire and forced us to
reinvent it. I would like to begin on a personal note.

In 1967, I began teaching in the English Department at the State University of New York at Buffalo,
which was, even then, in a particularly open relation
to Continental thought. The Hopkins conference[1]
had an immediate effect there, and as a result my first
year marked the loss of a certain innocence in my relation to the books I had to teach and write about. I
remember in the early 1960's, when I first entered
graduate school, one professor, in an offhand and dia-
bolical way, asked us on the opening day of class to
write a short essay on why we wanted to be professors
of literature. This produced the usual windy exercises
in bad faith, with one exception. The student sitting
next to me, with the absolute transparency of saints

[1] Published as *The Structuralist Controversy*, ed. Richard Macksey and
Eugenio Donato (Baltimore, Md., 1970).

and con artists, wrote simply, "I love to read books and to write about them."

I was taken by the beautiful simplicity of this statement, with its implicit description of a perfect circuit of desire from the reader's question through the author's response to the publication of their exchange. It controlled my imagination of my professional activity through the rest of graduate school, and when I started teaching I thought the repetition of this circuit would be my life. English Literature lay before me; each act of interpretation would be like an ideal date in which the expectation of analysis would lead to the consummate moment of understanding, which would, in turn, be certified by the essay that would inevitably follow.

The belief that a reader's conversation with and about a work could be characterized by this kind of transparency involves, of course, a certain persistent innocence. This is the same innocence that characterizes lovers in their initial address to the other. They, too, believe that they can elicit from this other a response that is adequate to their desire. Their "I love yous" demand an equally explicit "I love you, too" in return, a reply that simply mirrors and completes their question. In this sense, the critics of the American academy in the 1950's and 1960's could be said to share the impossible optimism of lovers. The methodology of the explication that dominated academic writing at this time was designed to resolve any ambivalences and contradictions within the work and allow it to reply to the critic with a coherence that would still the questioning desire that had drawn him to it. The lover contemplates the other's actions, speculates about the other's motive, interprets the flow of signs that the other produces, only to reach the moment when the other's "I love you, too" will resolve the issue. In the same way, these critics studied the ambiguity of a poem, its ironies, only to reach that moment when the explicit coherence of the reading resolved all ambivalences and ironies.

To become aware that you live in a fallen world is to become aware that this kind of correspondence between desire and its object, between question and response, is impossible. The force of the ideas classified under the name "structuralism" is, of course, to make this impossibility apparent in a way that has robbed critics of their ability to espouse such innocence easily. The happy marriage between critic and work that had been celebrated in the explication was shattered, and critics found themselves in the position of lovers who have begun to realize that there is something fundamentally mystified in their expectation that the other will or can complete their demand. In the face of this disillusionment, critics had a limited range of choices.

On the one hand, they could attempt to remain innocent and continue to ask the work to respond with a simple, single meaning. It is always possible, of course, to stage innocence in even the most unlikely places. Once, passing through southern Kansas in August, I was reading a Wichita newspaper and came across an account of a reporter's visit to the only nudist colony in the state. The reporter went expecting scenes of sexual liberation. Instead, she discovered a serious group of farmers and their wives who lectured her endlessly on the philosophy of nudism. Their innocence was a form of work performed among sun and briars. The paranoia, the marginality, and, finally, the failure that such efforts to establish a prelapsarian simplicity inevitably encounter were indicated by the sign on the gate which read: STOP. NUDIST COLONY. HONK FOR INFORMATION.

On the other hand, it would be equally possible for critics to embrace a disillusioned wisdom and turn their backs on literature the way disappointed lovers might turn their backs on all relations with the other and abandon their former desires.

The real issues, however, lie outside these two purely reactive positions. These issues center on what it means to continue to desire an other—either the other of the lover or the other of the poem—even after the realization that this other cannot respond. This involves neither the artificial preservation of innocence nor the acceptance of a "wisdom" that pretends to be beyond desire; rather, it requires the transformation of desire in relation to its initial object. Clearly, this transformation involves more than the persistence of desire in lovers or critics as a kind of lonely obsession. Both have sought a conversation with the other, with the text. Their desire for the other was a desire for a certain kind of exchange. The transformation of the relation between desire and the object, then, involves discovering another way of making their desire the subject of a conversation, another way of putting it into circulation. As different as they are, both Paul de Man's *The Resistance to Theory* and

Roland Barthes's *A Lover's Discourse* are concerned with this search.

In *The Resistance to Theory*,[2] de Man gives us three versions of the opposition between knowledge and innocence. The first tells the now familiar story of the conflict between the traditional academic establishment of the 1960's and the emergence of a true literary theory. The latter, according to de Man, can be said to come into being "when the approach to literary texts is no longer based on non-linguistic, that is to say historical or aesthetic, consideration or, to put it somewhat less crudely, when the object of discussion is no longer the meaning or the value but the modalities of production and of reception of meaning and of value prior to their establishment" (p. 7). Specifically, this moment corresponds to the introduction of a linguistic terminology into the metalanguage about literature, a terminology that considers "reference a function of language, not of intuition" (p. 8). This attention to the mode of production privileges the rhetorical and results in the discovery of what de Man calls the literariness of the text—a literariness that has nothing to do with aesthetics and everything to do with the revelation that the effective force of literature lies in its ability to represent rather than embody self and world.

Conceived in this way, literary theory has the power to unmask the false nature of convention, and this, in turn, explains for de Man the hostility of the

2 Paul de Man, *The Resistance to Theory* (Minneapolis, Minn., 1986). The essay giving its title to this work was first published in *Yale French Studies* in 1982.

traditional academic world toward such theory. Because it demystifies the expressive and descriptive powers of language, this theory attacks both the integrity of a social and historical self and the aesthetic categories that are the common assumption of the academic world.

This is only political resistance, however. The commitment of the academic establishment to a certain "innocent" meaning is only a commitment to its own conventional position. The commitment has no philosophic weight, and hence this first resistance has no real significance, although it can, of course, pose practical problems.

The dismissal of an external opposition, however, only reveals another, more profound issue. It may be, de Man continues, that this external opposition is only a function of a conflict within the theoretical enterprise itself. "The resistance to theory," he contends, "is a resistance to the use of language about language. It is, therefore, a resistance to language itself or to the possibility that language contains factors or functions that cannot be reduced to intuition" (pp. 12–13). This discomfort with the rhetorical as opposed to the semantic function of language has been a characteristic of literary thought throughout its history. For de Man, this is not a "modern" or "post-modern" problem, but a conflict that lies at the heart of the theoretician's project itself. In this context, resistance takes on a psychological overtone—that which defends the ego from a knowledge that has been repressed—and the argument becomes introspective. Literary theory is "overdetermined," its political opposition only "displaced symptoms" of its internal conflict, and this, in turn, requires a "self-analysis" by literary theory of its "insecurity" about its own project (p. 12).

Thus the real problem in literary theory lies in something that conflicts or frustrates the project of criticism internally. On one level, the terms of this conflict are clear. There is an opposition between the semantic and the rhetorical aspects of a text. Hence the critic who comes to the work to ask it for its meaning, and consequently is led to analyze its rhetorical structures, arrives, finally, at a "residue of indetermination that has to be, but cannot be, resolved by grammatical means, however extensively conceived" (p. 15). He finds, in other words, that the rhetorical undoes the promise of the grammatical or thematic.

But on another level the issue is not so clear, because there is something in the critic that resists this discovery, rejecting new knowledge in order to persist in his former innocence. The grounds for this continued resistance that conflicts the whole project of literary theory can be seen in the opposition between "has to" and "cannot be" in the phrase "a residue of indetermination that has to be, but cannot be, resolved." The critic is caught between an imperative and a hard place. The alternative is not a simple choice between an older, outmoded methodology and a new one; rather, it is an opposition between something the critic feels he "has to" do and something that tells him he "cannot" do it.

In a brief discussion of Keats's poem "The Fall of Hyperion," de Man dramatizes this conflict in unusually immediate terms. For de Man, the undecidability of Keats's poem is apparent in the very title of the work, in the critic's inability to determine whether the possessive "Hyperion's" refers to "the case story of the defeat of an older by a newer power, the very recognizable story from which Keats indeed started out but from which he increasingly strayed away, or [to] 'Hyperion falling,' the much less specific but more disquieting evocation of an actual process of falling, regardless of its beginning, its end, or the actual identity of the being to whom it befalls to be falling" (p. 16). This involves a number of complexities, but it is not, finally, an abstract issue. It is a question, in de Man's words, of "what the text actually does to us" (*ibid.*).

Faced with the ineluctable necessity to come to a decision, no grammatical or logical analysis can help us out. Just as Keats had to break off the narrative, the reader has to break off his understanding at the very moment when he is most directly engaged and summoned by the text. One could hardly expect to find solace in this "fearful symmetry" between the author's and the reader's plight since, at this point, the symmetry is no longer a formal but an actual trap, and the question no longer "merely" theoretical. (pp. 16–17)

We can see here that the resistance that exists within theory has to do with the persistence of that strong, naïve, "innocent" desire that first drew the critic to the work. The "ineluctable necessity" that drives the reader to analyze the poem—drives him to come to a decision—is, clearly, the same force that responds to the poem's summons. Both are the expressions of a desire for that single, unified meaning that is, finally, the figure of the author. This desire is not present only in the reader's early encounters with the work, before he has become theoretically sophisticated. Instead, de Man argues, the reader's desire continues to inhabit—and to resist from within—even the most sophisticated rhetorical theory. To read, then, is inevitably to desire and, just as inevitably, to fall, since the reader's questioning of the poem will ceaselessly return him to the point of undecidability.

From this point of view, the experience of falling—the experience of undecidability—can be characterized as an extreme state of isolation in which the critic is cut off from the communities that traditionally unite books and their readers. On the one hand, he is separated from the figure of the author—the unified meaning—that is the objective of his desire. True, critic and author are both trapped in a "fearful symmetry"; *both* are falling. But this symmetry is not a shared experience—that is, it is not recoverable as a common understanding—because it is a literal, not a figural, state. It is not a metaphor about the loss of meaning but the actual experience of this loss. Critic and author fall in parallel trajectories that never meet.

This isolation is only intensified when the critic looks up from the poem. Then he confronts the faces of his students and colleagues. If not always an eager audience, they are, we all know, a relentlessly expectant one. They await the product of the critic's analysis—the published paper, the lecture—and remind us that, within this profession, the reader's task is finished only when his determination of the poet's meaning is published and circulates as a form of knowledge. (We should remember, too, that this is not an extraneous issue in an essay like de Man's, which was originally intended for a review of research on critical theory but first published in a volume devoted to the relationship between teaching and theory.)

The critic, then, has both internal (psychological) and external reasons for resolving his resistance. The solution—which occupies the third and final movement of de Man's essay—is again provided by the "introduction of linguistic terminology into the metalanguage about literature" (p. 8). This terminology allows the critic to recover the experience of falling on the level of theory—to formulate it explicitly as a general law that determines the way literature produces the illusion of meaning. And this, in turn, can be extended to a rigorous method of reading texts in which the decoding, as opposed to the interpretation, is formalized as "a negative process in which the grammatical cognition is undone, at all times, by its rhetorical displacement" (p. 17).

The insistence on the thoroughness of this procedure, on the fact that the grammatical cognition must be undone *at all times*, is most obviously directed against the thematic level of the work. But its real target is clearly the critic's initial desire for this meaning. The thematic is posited only to be decoded, negated, the author revealed to be "dead." But to say that the author and his meaning are a dead issue is to say that the critic's desire for this meaning is a dead issue.

Thus the movement to theory is possible only if the critic continually searches for and extinguishes every manifestation of the desire that summoned him to the poem in the first place.

This pattern will be familiar to anyone who has read de Man's earlier piece, "The Rhetoric of Temporality,"[3] despite the many conceptual differences between the two essays. There, in his discussion of irony in Baudelaire's essay on laughter, de Man described the process of doubling that occurs in the philosopher when he encounters that most ordinary of accidents and falls down. At the moment of falling, the philosopher's consciousness splits into two distinct selves. One is an empirical self that is characterized by an illusory sense of superiority to nature and that falls as a result of this illusion. The other is an ironic consciousness that constitutes itself in the negation of the empirical self and that is characterized by its awareness of the former's mystification.

Similarly, in *The Resistance to Theory*, the critic's consciousness at the moment of falling is split between a naïve reader who, heavy with desire, trips on the grammatical level of the text, and an ironic, theoretical consciousness that exists in its negation of this reader and in its awareness of this reader's illusions. In "The Rhetoric of Temporality," this second, ironic position is completely unstable. The ironic consciousness is always tempted to come to the aid of the empirical self, to try to convert its own ironic wis-

[3] Paul de Man, "The Rhetoric of Temporality," reprinted in *Blindness and Insight* (Minneapolis, Minn., 1983), pp. 187–228. This essay was first published in 1969.

dom into a practical knowledge that could save the empirical self from falling. But this effort by the ironic to rejoin the empirical self always ends in another fall and, consequently, another ironic doubling. In the same way, the theoretician is always tempted to turn his awareness into an aid for the reader in the latter's quest for the poem's meaning, and can only master this temptation by a ceaseless repetition of the process of decoding in which grammatical cognition is undone and the theorist differentiated from the reader once again.

The critic moves from an attempt to interpret the work to a theory that allows him to decode the text. In doing so, he surrenders the desire that first attracted him to the poem. But in making this transition from reading to theory, he not so much abandons his desire as he transforms and completes it on another level. Initially, the critic explicates the poem in order to find himself in relation to an explicit and coherent meaning. Then, he discovers that this meaning is unrecoverable as a positive knowledge of the poem itself. It *is* recoverable, however, as a theory of the impossibility of this meaning. The "methodical undoing of the grammatical construct will be theoretically sound as well as effective," de Man tells us, and consequently, "technically correct rhetorical readings may be boring, monotonous, predictable and unpleasant, but they are irrefutable" (*Resistance*, p. 19).

The critic, then, can once again recover himself in an explicit knowledge that is universal, objective. For the lover, the explicitness of the other's "I love you, too" marks his possession of this other. For the critic who has become a theorist, the explicitness of the rhetorical reading also marks the possession of an other. This is not, of course, the other of the poem—the "author" and his meaning. This theory finds itself not in relation to the work but in relation to other critics. Its effectiveness is defined by its ability to refute and thereby possess other readers. Rhetorical readings, de Man continues, are "totalizing (and potentially totalitarian), for since the structures and functions they expose do not lead to the knowledge of an entity (such as language) but are an unreliable process of knowledge production that prevents all entities, including linguistic entities, from coming into discourse as such, they are indeed universals" (*ibid.*).

Because a rhetorical theory has this "totalizing (and potentially totalitarian)" power, it exists, finally, in its ability to control the exchanges around it, to conquer an audience and a discipleship. At this point, the "resistance" in *The Resistance to Theory* takes on a third implication. Here, it seems to refer to the power of such a rhetorical theory to resist all other forms of reading, and thus to command the field of critical discourse. It is not surprising, then, that in his third section de Man turns away from the frustration of the encounter with Keats's poem to confront once again the current critical scene (specifically, theories of reading) and to chastise them for their failure to problematize the act of reading itself.

One could say that it is in this movement from an addressing of the poem to a polemical confrontation with other critics that the theorist finds a mastery of the very desire that was frustrated by the undecidability of the poem itself. In this way, the imaginary of theory allows the critic to live his desire as something more than an isolated frustration. This transformation is, in this sense, the story behind *The Resistance to Theory*. It is also the story behind Barthes's *A Lover's Discourse*.[4] Here, too, the subject is drawn to an image of the other as the critic was drawn to the poem by the image of the author and his meaning. Again, the initial address to this image produces only frustration, ambivalence, and undecidability, which finally lead to a transformation in the relation between desire and its object.

Initially, the lover is "ravished" by an image (*Discourse*, p. 18). "By a singular logic, the amorous subject perceives the other as a Whole (in the fashion of Paris on an autumn afternoon)," and he is seized by "the notion, the hope, that the loved object will bestow itself upon [his] desire" (p. 19). This relationship may appear fetishistic to onlookers, but the lover does not experience it this way. He does not focus on some aspect of the loved object "without concern for the response [since] like God . . . the fetish does not reply" (p. 67). He is not perverse: "He is in love. He creates meaning everywhere," and consequently, "every contact for the lover raises the question of an answer" (*ibid.*).

The lover is summoned by the promise of a response; he seeks a reply that will answer the question of his desire. But this question is only the question of

4 Roland Barthes, *A Lover's Discourse* (New York, 1978).

his own ultimate meaning. "I look for signs, but of what? What is the object of my reading? . . . Isn't it . . . that I remain suspended on this question, whose answer I tirelessly seek in the other's face: 'What am I worth?'" (p. 214). The lover wants to know the other in a way that will return him to himself. But he finds himself engaged in a ceaseless interpretation that leads nowhere. "A man who wants the truth is never answered save in strong, highly colored images, which nonetheless turn ambiguous, indecisive, once he tries to transform them into signs" (p. 215).

The lover's situation is, by nature, then, an indecisive one. He will never extract from the other a reply that is adequate to his question, and finally his awareness of the endless frustration that lies before him leads him to "break off the effort at understanding" (*Resistance*, p. 16). He surrenders the project of reassembling Plato's hermaphrodite—that is, the "natural" and "instinctive" search for an other who will be the complement of his desire. This "figure of that ancient unity of which the desire and the pursuit constitute what we call 'love' is beyond my figuration; or at least all I could ever achieve is a monstrous, grotesque improbable body. Out of the dream emerges the farce figure: thus out of the mad couple is born the obscenity of the household (one cooks for life, for the other)" (*Discourse*, p. 227). The "loved being becomes a leaden figure, a dream creature who does not speak, and silence, in dreams, is death" (p. 168).

The silence of the other is only intensified by the lover's alienation from any larger social context.

There is, of course, the identification among lovers themselves, the "chain of equivalences" that "links all the lovers in the world" (p. 131). But this linkage is of a particularly narrow kind. Lovers identify with one another, but only if they are passing through the same moment or figure of love at exactly the same time. To the jealous lover, for example, the happy lover is a fool; to the happy lover, the jealous lover is a paranoid. They only identify if they can find themselves imaged in the other in a one-to-one correspondence. Otherwise, they see only absolute difference. There is no comprehensive understanding.

The same applies to the lover's conventional, social world of men and women—former and future lovers—who, for the time being, stand at some remove from desire. They, too, look upon the lover as an alien.

Theory could possibly bridge this gap between the lover and the surrounding world—that is, it could provide an understanding of the lover that is not dependent on an immediate identification with him. But no such theoretical language exists; all available theories treat the lover from a position of objectivity and, consequently, reduce him to a symptom. They deny him understanding on his own terms. Thus he is "exiled from all gregarity," he is mad "not because [he] is original but because [he] is severed from all sociability" (p. 121). He is atopic; he has no place.

It is the lover's arrival at this radical solitude, alone with the peculiarity of a desire that isolates him both from others and from *the* other, that gives rise to *A Lover's Discourse*. Arrival at this point is marked by a crisis that is the subject of the fragment entitled "I want to understand": "Suddenly perceiving the amorous episode as a knot of inexplicable reasons and impaired solutions, the subject exclaims 'I want to understand (what is happening to me)!'" (p. 59). The lover, realizing that his situation is unresolvable in the terms in which it "naturally" appears to him, hopes to analyze it, to comprehend it in a way that will change his relation to it. But there is a problem: "What I want to know (love) is the very substance I employ in order to speak (the lover's discourse)" (*ibid.*). As a result, the lover has no distance on himself. He is "excluded from logic, which supposes languages exterior to each other" and "cannot claim to think properly" (*ibid.*).

The obvious answer is for the lover to adopt one or another metalanguage that would supply the necessary escape to an outside. Psychology would allow him to understand his love as a relationship to a fetishized image; rhetorical theory would demystify representation. Each would offer him a way to interpret his love that would free him from it, allow him to master it.

The lover is tempted.

Repression: I want to analyze, to know, to express myself in another language than mine; I want to represent my delirium to myself, I want to "look in the face" what is dividing me, cutting me off. *Understand your madness*: that was Zeus's command when he ordered Apollo to turn the faces of the divided Androgynes . . . toward the place where they had been cut apart "so that the sight of this division might make them less insolent." To understand—is that not to divide the image, to undo the *I*, the proud organ of misapprehension? (p. 60)

But he immediately rejects this alternative.

Interpretation. No, that is not what your cry [I want to understand] means. As a matter of fact, that cry is still a cry of love: I want to understand myself, to make myself understood, to make myself known. (p. 59)

This rejection of the movement to a place outside desire, from which analysis usually takes place, can be understood in several ways. But the most obvious is offered in the fragment "Adorable." "*Adorable* means: this is my desire, insofar as it is unique. 'That's it! That's it, exactly (which I love)!'" (p. 20). The lover's madness is not an alienation from his "real" self. "For me as an amorous subject it is the contrary: . . . I am indefectibly myself, and it is in this that I am mad" (p. 121). The amorous interlude, in other words, has revealed a truth beneath an illusion. The illusion is the imagination of an other with the power to answer. The truth is the desire itself, which is born in this other's cataclysmic effect on the lover. In one of the footnotes to his discussion of Plato's hermaphrodite, Barthes quotes a maxim of Jacques Lacan that "psychoanalysis seeks the missing organ (the libido) and not the missing half" (p. 226). The power of love is that it performs the work of analysis; that is, it discovers our libido and makes us experience our true desire.

Love makes us experience this desire. But it does not allow us to know it or name it. "Yet at the same time *adorable* says everything: it also says what is lacking in everything; it seeks to designate that site of the other to which my desire clings in a special way, but this site cannot be designated; about it I will never know anything" (p. 19). Love gives us to ourselves, then, but it gives us to ourselves as an endless experience of desiring until death, an experience that can never, in and of itself, be recuperated as a meaning, as a conversation or exchange with an other.

Nevertheless, the lover must choose the truth of his desire, even in the face of its inevitable frustration. "To be in the truth, it is enough to persist: a lure endlessly affirmed, against everything, becomes a truth" (p. 230). He must maintain his desire while abandoning the will to possess, to interpret, to know, that attempts to realize this desire.

The lover, then, denies himself the alternative that saves the critic in de Man's *The Resistance to Theory*. He wants to understand, but rejects an understanding that completes itself at the level of a theory of love that would relentlessly demonstrate its illusions. Such an understanding would inevitably lead to *A Lover's Discourse*, which was a polemic against lovers and which worked to master them by demonstrating irrefutably the mystified nature of their pursuit. In other words, the lover rejects the explicit analysis of love in terms of some other language that would inevitably be experienced by both reader and author as the latter's theoretical mastery. But at the same time, the lover cannot simply continue to write the "natural" expression of his feeling. This would return him to the initial situation of lovers, although to remain

silent would be to live his feelings in a pointless isolation.

The lover, then, must find a way to write with desire *and* understanding. The larger question, of
course, is how to write about anything that truly at-
tracts our desire without, on the one hand, succumbing to the illusion of that attraction—which seems to
promise the real possession of the object—or, on the
other, surrendering to the seductions of a theory that
seems to allow us to escape frustration in an explicit
understanding of this illusion, but that does so at the
expense of the specificity of our desire itself. Yet how
is it possible to speak and think—to understand and
make understood—the lover's position in such an
ambivalent way?

The opening section of *A Lover's Discourse* tells us
that the author has chosen a "'dramatic' method" (p.
3) that renounces examples and "rests on the single
action of a primary language (no metalanguage)"
(*ibid.*) in which we can hear "what is 'unreal,' i.e., in-
tractable" (p. 37) in the lover's voice. It gives us, then,
the unmediated expression of desire itself. It is not a
work "about" desire in which the lover would be "reduced to a simple symptomal subject" (p. 3), but one
that accepts—affirms—this experience on its own
terms. And insofar as it does present the lover's experience in such an unmediated way, it offers the
reader a certain identification with this experience.
The affirmation of love here implies to some degree
the affirmation of this kind of sympathetic embrace
by the reader of the lover and his story.

But although *A Lover's Discourse* does offer us

these moments, it is not just a straightforward dramatization. If it were, it would simply double Goethe's *The Sorrows of Young Werther*, which is, Barthes tells us, the "pure discourse of the amorous subject" (p. 211). The complete portrait is not "psychological" but "structural" (p. 3). The lover is not a natural figure. He is produced at the intersection of desire and culture; "he 'phrases,' like an orator; he is caught, stuffed into a role, like a statue" (p. 4). His desire, displaced into language, is structured by this language. It will inevitably find itself an "I" addressing a "you," from whom it will be separated by an unbridgeable distance. More than this, the particular form of address will be determined by the current conventions of the culture. "What passes through (the lover's) mind at a certain moment is *marked*, like the printout of a code (in other times this would have been the code of courtly love or the Carte du Tendre)" (p. 4).

The lover, then, is a "good cultural subject" (*ibid.*), but he does not see that what appears to him to be the "naturalness" of his experience is, in fact, the action of conventional laws. *A Lover's Discourse*, however, stages or "simulates" the dramatic moments of this story so that the actions of these laws are apparent. The instruments of this distancing are, again, not the overt mechanisms of a metalanguage but various strategies of alienation that obviously derive, at least in part, from Barthes's interest in Brecht. Although moments are dramatized, the narrative of the lover is broken, fragmented, and rearranged arbitrarily (alphabetically) to counteract the psychological identification that narrative promotes. Each fragment is preceded by a brief statement of the argument, "instrument of distancing, signboard à la Brecht" (p. 5), that calls attention precisely to what is topical (that is, not personal) in the lover's utterance. On the one hand, each fragment, or figure, is like a physical gesture. "These fragments of discourse can be called figures. The word is to be understood, not in its rhetorical sense, but rather in its gymnastic or choreographic acceptation . . . the body gesture caught in action, not contemplated in repose" (pp. 3–4). On the other hand, "figures take shape insofar as we can recognize, in passing discourse, something that has been read, heard, felt. . . . A figure is established if at least someone can say 'That's so true! I recognize that scene of language!'" (p. 4). Like Brecht's social gestus, then, the figure shows us, in the action of one, the "gestural expression of the social relationships prevailing between people."[5]

In *A Lover's Discourse*, we are given both the experience of love and a way of reading this experience that reveals the mechanisms of its production. We might think for a moment about the way this juxtaposition of identification and alienation works in the fragment entitled, appropriately, "Identifications." The previous fragment ends with the invocation of Werther's blue coat and yellow vest, which he had worn when he first danced with Charlotte, in which he was buried, and which subsequently became a "perverse outfit . . . worn across Europe by the nov-

5 John Willett, ed., *Brecht on Theatre* (New York, 1964), p. 133.

el's enthusiasts and . . . known as a 'costume à la Werther!'" (*Discourse*, p. 128). This fragment begins on the same note. "Werther identifies himself with every lost lover: he is the madman who loved Charlotte and goes out picking flowers in midwinter; he is the young footman in love with a widow, who kills his rival" (p. 129). What is evoked here is the intensely personal, dramatic identification between lovers who are undergoing a similar moment.

Werther identifies himself with the madman, with the footman. As a reader, I can identify myself with Werther. Historically, thousands of subjects have done so, suffering, killing themselves. . . . In the theory of literature, "projection" (of the reader into the character) no longer has any currency; yet it is the appropriate tonality of imaginative readings: reading a love story, it is scarcely adequate to say I project myself; I cling to the image of the lover, shut up with this image in the very enclosure of the book (everyone knows that such stories are read in a state of retirement, of voluptuous absence, in the toilet). (p. 131)

Although this imaginative identification with the lover's story seems to unite lovers, it is really only another way each experiences his own isolation (wearing the costume à la Werther, the "blue garment imprisons [the lover] so effectively that the world around him vanishes" [p. 128]; reading *Werther*, the lover is locked up with himself in a state of "voluptuous absence" in the "enclosure" [p. 131] of the book, of the toilet). Against this form of dramatic identification, then, the fragment places another understanding of identification that sees that it is "not a psychological process [but] a pure structural operation: I am the one who has the same place I have" (p. 129). From this perspective,

I devour every amorous system with my gaze and in it discover the place which would be mine if I were a part of that system. I perceive not analogies but homologies: I note, for instance, that I am to X what Y is to Z; everything I am told about Y affects me powerfully, though Y's person is a matter of indifference to me. . . . I am caught in a mirror which changes position and which reflects me wherever there is a dual position. (p. 129)

This ability to read the structure of mimetic desire behind the dramatic surface of the amorous situation creates an "I" who escapes the claustrophobia of the lover's absolutely immediate and personal experience. (This "I" no longer believes that the situation of rivalry with Y is a result of their personal narrative, that it is something that Y has chosen to do to him.) Instead, he realizes that "the structure has nothing to do with persons; hence (like a bureaucracy) it is terrible. It cannot be implored—I cannot say to it: 'Look how much better I am than H.' Inexorable, the structure replies, 'You are in the same place; hence you *are* H'" (p. 130).

Because it is not narrowly personal, in the sense that Werther's narrative is, the "I" who defines each figure is open to readers outside a single psychological identification. Each figure defines a topic, and

the property of a topic is to be somewhat empty. A topic is statutorily half coded, half projective (or projective because coded). What we have been able to say below about waiting, anxiety, memory is no more than a modest supplement to be added to or subtracted from, passed to others: around the figure, the players pass the handkerchief which sometimes, by a final parenthesis, is held a second longer before handing it on. (Ideally, the book would be a cooperative: "To the United Readers and Lovers"). (p. 5)

This "I," which sees itself as just another letter designating a position in a structure, can phrase its experience so that it has the accessibility of a theoretical formulation. It is this accessibility that creates the larger community of readers and lovers—larger and more comprehensive than the claustrophobic identification of the lover with Werther.

From this perspective, what is most striking about *A Lover's Discourse* is Barthes's use of a certain theoretical perspective to create the rhetorical space of the figure or topic. In other words, what is most striking is not what is personal in the book but what is impersonal, what is coded in such a way that we can read in it not the immediacy but the pattern of our own experience. This does not mean, however, that the "I" who speaks in "Identifications" is beyond desire, that its knowledge of the triangular structure of desire frees it from the situation. Just the opposite.

Worse still: it can happen that on the other hand I am loved by someone I do not love; now [that I understand the structure of identification] far from helping me (by the gratification it implies or the diversion it might constitute), this situation is painful to me: I see myself in the other who loves without being loved, I recognize in him the very gestures of my own unhappiness, but this time it is myself who am the active agent of this unhappiness: I experience myself both as victim and executioner. (p. 130)

The act of reading only opens up the structure in such a way that the reader can identify in turn with each figure, be both victim and executioner.

The result, both for the reader and for the "I" who speaks in the book, is a kind of ambivalence—the "consciousness of unconsciousness" that Barthes described as the effect of Brecht's theater.

Here, too, the audience *knows* what the actor does not know; and upon seeing him act so harmfully and so stupidly, the audience is amazed, disturbed, indignant, shouts out the truth, one step more and the spectator will see that the suffering and ignorant actor is himself. . . . It is therefore crucial that this theatre never completely implicate the audience in the spectacle: if the spectator does not keep that slight distance necessary in order to see himself suffering and mystified, all is lost: the spectator must partly identify himself [with the dramatic character] and espouse [his] blindness only to withdraw from it in time and to judge it.[6]

This double consciousness allows the lover to both be and know his madness and, in doing so, to share it with others.

Like the theorist, in other words, the lover can have the relief of conversation. If we step back for a moment and look at both *The Resistance to Theory* and *A Lover's Discourse* from this point of view, what seems most important is the difference between the

[6] Roland Barthes, "Mother Courage Blind," in *Critical Essays* (Evanston, Ill., 1972), p. 34.

tone of these two conversations. In one way, of course, both are about the same subject. We can see now that the real effect of the "demystification" of the relation between the reader and the work and between the lover and the beloved has been to return the subject's desire to him. This is obvious in the case of de Man but no less true for Barthes. The situation of a desire that has been detached from its initial, "natural" object and returned to the subject is the problem addressed by both works. It is a problem—as opposed to a release, for example—because, liberated from the shelter of a satisfaction or a meaning, desire is also liberated from the authority of this satisfaction or meaning. The reader and the lover's desire is returned to them. But it has no intrinsic or extrinsic value. It is just their desire, untransformed by any totalized significance, and, as such, it is insignificant. But since conversation is their only outlet now, each is faced with the task of making his desire interesting to others, something worth talking about.

A rhetorically based theory does this by sacrificing desire and recuperating this sacrifice as a powerful universal language that can command the respect and attention of the critical community, which must listen and respond. Its adherents are united by this language spoken by all its believers, and by the impact their language has on its opponents.

The Barthesian lover retains this desire—accepts the responsibility of its insignificance. He does not try to be explicitly powerful and avoids, too, the anger inspired by frustration. He makes himself seductive. "What if," the "I" of *A Lover's Discourse* asks, "it were asked of analysis not to destroy power (not even to correct or direct it) but only to decorate it, as an artist?" (p. 202). So the lover / reader decorates his desire, makes it the centerpiece of an "amiable" (p. 5) conversation that he hopes others will want to join, though he is aware all the time that if others do not find him attractive there is no way to mitigate this judgment.

As different as these two exchanges seem, they do have one characteristic in common. Both the reiteration of a theory among its adherents (and the arguments this reiteration provokes) and the reminiscences of lovers are frequently forms of distraction. Both are the kinds of conversations we have when we have nothing else to do, or when we are frustrated at not being able to do what we have to do. We engage in them to make ourselves slightly more comfortable when we have to pass the time.

From this point of view, the most relevant commentary on the situation is provided by Joseph Conrad's *Lord Jim*. In this novel, a young Englishman pursues a particularly exaggerated and heroic image of himself. In the face of a series of failures that demonstrate the incoherence of both his own personality and the world around him, he persists in the most innocent form of this search with a formidable energy until it leads, finally, to his death.

Jim's case is presented to us by two different narrators. The first is detached, "objective," and judgmental. He sees Jim as a fool who refuses to recognize the nature of illusion. The second is a former seaman, Marlow, who remembers his own dreams and is more understanding and involved. He tries to make a case for Jim and to present Jim's persistence in the face of failure as a form of heroism in itself.

But Marlow is disillusioned enough not to persist himself. He and his friends discuss Jim's situation over brandy and cigars after a fine dinner. They are sitting in easy chairs on the veranda of a hotel overlooking the harbor. Similarly, the objective narrator has withdrawn to the safety of an Olympian detachment from which he can watch and judge the efforts of those beneath him. In the complicated imagistic structure of the novel, this kind of withdrawal to an elevated position is associated with a withdrawal into a passive ease. Both narrators, in other words, have found ways to make themselves comfortable in the face of Jim's figure.

It is Barthes himself who has said the final word on this process of making oneself comfortable. In *Barthes by Barthes*, he remembers a grandfather who, crippled by advancing age, had a little platform built so that he could see out the window from his bed. This acquiescence to an inevitable limitation and "surrender of all heroism (even in pleasure)"[7] marks, for Barthes, the ethical dimension of ease. From this perspective, we can see the essential structure of the comfortable. It is something we give ourselves in compensation for a greater loss. Lose your leg; improve your view.

[7] Roland Barthes, *Barthes by Barthes* (New York, 1977), pp. 43–44.

Nostalgia and Critical Theory

Josué Harari

T he success of theory in academic circles need no longer be emphasized. It
is clearly evident in the number of symposia, articles,
journals, departments, and even entire "schools" that
specialize in theory. Yet it is this very proliferation
that has induced Stanley Fish to proclaim the immi-
nent demise of theory, a demise whose most telling
symptom is precisely the "noise" generated by theory.[1] Commenting on and extending Fish's line of argument, Vincent Descombes argues that we have entered a phase of theoretical confusionism that makes
it difficult to determine what theory is.[2] To the above
two commentaries we should add a third, concerning
the "physiological" status of theory. I believe that
within the register of theory—as within the register
of wine and fine cuisine—there exists a scale of effects. Theory has its own range of degrees, which go

[1] Stanley Fish, "Consequences," *Critical Inquiry*, 11 (1985), 3.

[2] "For example, the thought of Jacques Derrida which, in France, is considered a difficult metaphysical inquiry, is held in the United States to be
a paradoxical theory of reading applicable to any text whatsoever." Vincent Descombes, "Les mots de la tribu," *Critique*, 456 (1985), 421–22.

from exaltation to torpor, and a good deal of the power of theory depends on this scale. Unfortunately, we have reached the point at which the excitement over the initial effects of theory is in the process of turning into its opposite: the ennui that comes from repetition. The result is a kind of theoretical monotony that is being acclaimed noblesse oblige, as a mark of intellectual snobbery.

One caveat is in order. It is my intention to advocate neither a complete return to "old-fashioned" criticism nor a rejection of theory, but rather to attempt to rediscover the early moments of theory— the moments when we are not bored, when we are under the spell of the surprise and excitement that come with first discovery. One might well ask whether such an enterprise is still possible after all the theoretical excesses to which we have been exposed in the last decade. The question becomes even more pertinent if one believes, as I do, that it is the very "advances" of theory (and the super-sophisticated concepts it has yielded) that are blurring our present attempts to understand what theory is. Indeed, the theoretical presuppositions with which we work have built up a store of knowledge at the very heart of theory that is completely out of proportion to the texts that theory claims to clarify; in consequence, theory has become essentially a repeated commentary on its own discourse. Breaking up the "monopoly" held by theoretical discourse on itself would require a general remodeling of our theoretical configuration. Montesquieu used the surprised eyes of two (supposedly naïve) Persian travelers to establish the distance necessary to make his commentary on French society. Based on this model, a (supposedly naïve) return to the "beginnings" of theory might produce an effect of surprise, that is, a *series of divergences* vis-à-vis the strict exigencies of today's theoretical discourse—divergences that could help us understand the constitution and function of (a) theory from its moment of inception. Let me illustrate this suggestion by way of an example.

The modern controversy that has taken place between Claude Lévi-Strauss and Jacques Derrida about the question of writing is well known. The reader certainly recalls the famous "Writing Lesson"[3] in which Lévi-Strauss relates the scene of the Nambikwara Indian chief who acts out the "comedy" of writing in order to appropriate power. Lévi-Strauss's analysis of this episode leads him to conclude that deviousness and violence accompany the "advent" of writing among Nambikwara Indians.[4] On the basis of this conclusion, he develops his thesis of the exploitation of man by man through writing.

Derrida takes this same Nambikwara episode as a point of departure in *Of Grammatology*,[5] in order to demonstrate that Lévi-Strauss's ethnological dis-

[3] Claude Lévi-Strauss, *Tristes Tropiques*, trans. John and Doreen Weightman (New York, 1974), pp. 294–304.

[4] "Writing and deceit had penetrated simultaneously in their midst" (*Tristes Tropiques*, p. 300).

[5] Jacques Derrida, "The Violence of the Letter: From Lévi-Strauss to Rousseau," in *Of Grammatology*, trans. G. Spivak (Baltimore, Md., 1976), pp. 101–40.

course is produced according to concepts and values integral to Occidental metaphysics, a metaphysics that invokes the fall into evil after the primordial innocence of the Verb. According to Derrida, if writing can be said to embody the ethical instance of violence, it is not, as Lévi-Strauss would like us to believe, the result of an outside violence that imposes itself on an inherent natural goodness characteristic of a people without writing. Derrida's brilliant theoretical development rests on two interrelated points: (1) the Nambikwara writing lesson does not represent a scene of the "birth" of writing, but is only an instance of its mimetic importation; and (2) corruption existed among the Nambikwara Indians long before writing's advent, hence violence is not an exclusive quality of writing (as opposed to the innocence of speech). Let me stop for a moment here and, in counterpoint to the Lévi-Strauss/Derrida theoretical debate, recount a fictional version of the advent of writing. It appears in an *Abrégé de toutes les sciences à l'usage des enfants* dating back to 1790. In response to the question "Who invented writing?" asked in the chapter on "Languages," the child is told an Indian myth that I quote in its entirety:

The *Hebrews*, struck by the wonder of the art, called it *Dikduk*, that is, subtle invention. The *Americans* at first believed that paper could speak, upon seeing someone read from a book.

There is a story told about an Indian slave who, having been entrusted by his master with a basket of figs and a letter to be sent to an acquaintance, ate a portion of the figs along the way, and gave the rest along with the letter to his master's friend. When he read the letter and discovered that it promised a greater quantity of figs than he had actually received, the master's friend accused the slave of having eaten the missing figs, and read to him the contents of the letter. Yet the Indian swore that it was not so, cursed the letter and accused it of bearing false witness.

A few days later, the slave was charged with a similar task, with a letter that indicated the precise number of figs that he was to transport. As he was walking, he again ate some of the figs; but this time, in order to avoid being accused as he had been earlier, he took the precaution of hiding the letter under a big rock beforehand, and then felt assured that if the letter did not see him eat the figs, it could not tattle on him. Yet upon reaching his destination, the slave was berated more severely than ever; the poor fool ended by confessing his deed, and from that point on he bowed down in awe and admiration before the magical power of writing.[6]

This is a very pretty tale: each element corresponds to a recognized function of writing as described in the Lévi-Straussian version—hierarchization, exploitation, violence, economic power, inclusion of its holders in a quasi-religious secret. And yet this story also corresponds to the Derridian critique of writing. We see, openly here, that the elements of exploitation on the one hand, and of corruption and deviousness on the other, *precede* writing; and that in the end writing functions as *pharmakos*—a violent corrective to the

[6]*Abrégé*, edition revised and corrected by M. Varney (Paris, 1790), pp. 35–36.

violence of corruption. This short story illustrates the contemporary controversy of writing more effectively than any explanation offered by the most talented professor, even if he undertook to explain all of *Tristes Tropiques* and *Of Grammatology*. This is not to be construed as a reproach to Lévi-Strauss or Derrida, because I believe both authors would agree that if each had dreamed up a fiction to illustrate his respective theory of writing, he could have invented no more fitting a scenario.

Bricolage, or *différance* and *supplément*, comprise theory as it is currently understood; but what can we say about the tale of the Indian and his reaction to the advent of writing? Strictly speaking, the Indian has no theory of writing; consequently, he can only formulate an inadequate interpretation for what writing is or accomplishes.[7] However, had this Indian been promoted to the rank of modern theorist, he probably would have produced out of this scenario both Lévi-Strauss's theory of writing and its Derridian critique. The main point of my argument is that the Indian—as layman or as theorist—*does not draw his scenario out of a theory, but instead does just the opposite*: the scenario comes first and the theory, when there is one, follows, just as Lévi-Strauss's theory of writing is grounded in the Nambikwara writing scenario, and Derrida's critique is grounded in Lévi-Strauss's fictionalization of this scenario. In epistemological

[7] With respect to the act of interpretation, the Indian who has no theory does the same thing, but in reverse, as the critic who knows nothing but theory, and who, likewise, cannot interpret any further than to repeat a theory and all its related suppositions.

terms, the question is how it happens that, in litera-ture and in the human sciences, theory imposes itself as theory. A first answer is to look for a supporting sce-nario, for I would argue that underlying every theory there is a corresponding scenario, real or imaginary. In general, we critics fervently want to believe that we deduce interpretation from theory; yet the over-whelming evidence shows that theory is merely the justification, *after the fact*, of a scenario—in most cases a personal scenario—that imposes itself on an author for reasons that may or may not be related to the substance of the resulting theory.

In keeping with this view of the nature of theory, I would like to consider Lévi-Strauss's theory of struc-tural anthropology, in order to uncover the generative phantasms that underlie it, and thereby to "diagnose" those moments when the fictional scenario catches on and becomes theory. More precisely, I wish to ana-lyze how, at a theoretical level, when the most un-solvable problem about the nature of structuralist knowledge abruptly confronts Lévi-Strauss, it is only by means of an imaginary production that he suc-ceeds in resolving it. In other words, structuralism, or rather structural anthropology, has its point of depar-ture neither in anthropological reality nor in anthro-pological experience, but in a particular production of the Lévi-Straussian unconscious—an imaginary sce-nario that I shall attempt to bring to light through a reading of one chapter of *Tristes Tropiques* entitled "The Apotheosis of Augustus." But first, a brief meth-odological parenthesis.

In the crucial Chapter 6 of *Tristes Tropiques* ("The Making of an Anthropologist"), in which Lévi-Strauss explains his choice of a profession, he describes the role that his "three mistresses," as he calls them— Freud, Marx, and Geology—played in shaping structuralism's fundamental objective:

All three demonstrate that understanding consists in reducing one type of reality to another; that the true reality is never the most obvious; and that the nature of truth is already indicated by the care it takes to remain elusive. In all cases, the same problem arises from the problem of the relationship between feeling [*le sensible*] and reason [*le rationnel*], and the aim is the same: to achieve a kind of superrationalism, which will integrate the first with the second, without sacrificing any of its properties. (pp. 57–58)

But beyond this new definition of knowledge, the three mistresses raise the same problem. All three disciplines begin with situations of disorder—the human psyche, social upheaval, a rugged landscape— and yet the astute observer will recognize that beneath those surface incoherencies there is an intelligible order that is neither arbitrary nor contingent, but rather the result of a different kind of knowledge: "It was a quest which would have seemed incoherent to some uninitiated observer, but which I look upon as the very image of knowledge" (p. 56). This new order of knowledge is attained in all three disciplines through a logical model independent of reality: "The object is to construct a model and to study its property and its different reactions under laboratory conditions in order later to apply the observations to the interpretation of empirical happenings, which may be far removed from what had been forecast" (p. 57).[8] Thus for Lévi-Strauss intelligibility is not given at the level of perception or of daily experience; the meaning that must be abandoned is precisely that which is immediately experienced or perceived at the phenomenal level. This can be explained by the fact that, for Lévi-Strauss, it is never a question of having the model *correspond* to reality, but only of determining whether the model available is the best one for grasping reality—the nature of this reality remaining elusive, and for good reasons, as we shall see.

Ruffled Feathers

Readers of *Tristes Tropiques* undoubtedly remember "The Apotheosis of Augustus," the dramatic fable that concludes the final section of the book ("The Return"). The setting at Campos Novos is worth recalling. Lévi-Strauss is tired, discouraged, openly depressed. He finds himself separated from his companions (who have been immobilized by an epidemic), alone in the midst of two enemy Indian tribes who are

[8] For instance, when discussing the notion of social structure, Lévi-Strauss does not hesitate to ignore social customs, facts, and relationships, to the benefit of the conceptual coherence of the model: "It is hopeless to expect a structural analysis to change our way of perceiving concrete social relations. It will only explain them better. . . . But, if a distinction is made between the level of observation and symbols to be substituted to it, I fail to see why an algebraic treatment of, let us say symbols for marriage rules, could not teach us, when aptly manipulated, something about the way a given marriage system actually works and bring out properties not immediately apparent to the empirical observer." "The Meaning and Use of the Notion of Model," in *Structural Anthropology*, vol. 2, trans. M. Layton (New York, 1976), p. 80.

fighting each other and who "were not particularly well-disposed towards me. I had to keep a sharp lookout and all anthropological work became virtually impossible" (p. 375).

Lévi-Strauss is about to question the entire anthropological edifice: Does one become an ethnologist as a result of one's profound incompatibility with one's own social group, or is this nothing but a maneuver aimed at advancing one's career by exotic means? Is anthropology the product of an existential choice or of a vocation? Or is it a ruse by means of which one marks and flaunts one's difference from one's fellow citizens? The internal crisis provokes in Lévi-Strauss a state of corporeal trance that is coupled with sharp intellectual acuity. He is kept awake by this mental activity; images of paintings, sentences swarm in his head; he is in the grip of great instability and mental anguish. Suddenly, one afternoon, amid the horrendous heat, unbreathable air, and all-encompassing silence of the Mato Grosso, the imaginary scenario propels itself onto the scene of his unconscious: "I had the idea that the problems bothering me could provide the subject-matter of a play. It was as clear in my mind as if it had already been written" (p. 378). Without fully attempting to understand the meaning of the psychodrama he is experiencing, Lévi-Strauss transcribes its content. The finished product is so clearly defined in his unconscious that he knows the whole play before writing it, "as if it had already been written." Thus he goes on transcribing, transcribing, and transcribing: "For six days, I wrote from morning till night on the backs of sheets of paper covered with word lists, sketches and genealogical tables. After which, inspiration abandoned me before the work was completed, and has never returned since" (*ibid.*).[9]

What is remarkable during this whole episode is that the type of quasi-hallucinatory delirium that Lévi-Strauss underwent did not bring about any disturbance in his thinking. He entered a state of self-observation, becoming a doubled personality even more acutely conscious than he would normally be of all that is going through his mind. In any event, the episode concludes, to Lévi-Strauss's great surprise— is it really a surprise?—on a particularly pleasing note: "On rereading my scribblings, I don't think there is any cause for regret" (*ibid.*). Of course, Lévi-Strauss only means that he has no regrets about the aesthetic quality of the play produced by his unconscious. Yet he should also have no regrets about "The Apotheosis" on more than mere aesthetic grounds, for, as we shall see, this play constitutes the *manuel de défense et illustration* of structuralism in anthropology.

The play, which is offered as a new version of Corneille's *Cinna*, presents two childhood friends, Augustus and Cinna, who each personify one aspect of the unresolved "anthropological" dilemma that confronts Lévi-Strauss—and anthropology in general. Cinna is a social renegade "who thought he had opted out of civilization, and who discovers that he has used a complicated means of returning to it, but by a method destructive of the meaning and value of the

---

[9] The "creation" of structural anthropology, like God's universe, takes six days to be completed.

choice with which he had originally believed himself to be faced" (*ibid.*); Augustus is the representative of society who understands that "all of his efforts have been strained towards an end which dooms them to oblivion" (*ibid.*)

The play opens on a decree from the Roman senate to elevate Augustus to the rank of God. Soon thereafter Camille, Augustus's sister, announces the return of Cinna after ten years of life in the jungle. While pondering the meaning of the honor that he himself is about to receive, Augustus is torn over whether or not to see his childhood friend once again. Camille, who is in love with Cinna, urges Augustus to do so, "since she hoped that Cinna's wayward and poetic disposition, which had always been in evidence, would prevent Augustus from opting irrevocably for conventional social regimentation [*verser du côté de l'ordre*]" (p. 379). Lydia, Augustus's wife, is against such a meeting, because Cinna has always spelled trouble for her husband: "Cinna had always exercised a disruptive influence [*un élément de désordre*] on Augustus's career" (*ibid.*). (Let us keep in mind this opposition of Cinna/Augustus = disorder/ order, for my interpretation of the play will hinge on the transformation that this opposition undergoes.) Throughout the course of these discussions, Augustus has a tête-à-tête with a mythological eagle who explains to him the meaning of his impending divinity:

Augustus would realize that he had become a god, not by some radiant sensation or the power to work miracles, but by his ability to tolerate the proximity of a wild beast without a sensation of disgust, to put up with its stench and the excrement with which it would cover him. Carrion, decay and organic secretions would become familiar to him: "Butterflies will come and copulate on your neck and any kind of ground will seem good enough to sleep on." (pp. 379–80)

One can justifiably consider the eagle's speech as one of several variants on the great narrative of nature. The eagle affirms the impure and antisocial aspect, the inherent ambivalence, of the sacred, which can be just as easily malevolent as benevolent. In this light, filth and impurity (the central elements of the eagle's discourse) designate more than something dirty or disgusting. Rather, they embody nature's anarchic qualities—its variable and unpredictable manifestations, its web of incoherencies, its confusionism; in sum, the fundamental undifferentiation that characterizes nature. Thus Augustus will enter into the domain of the sacred not as an individual, that is, as *difference*, but rather as a supplement of impurity that will add itself to all other natural impurities: "Carrion, decay and organic secretion [will] become familiar to [you]: 'Butterflies will come and copulate on your neck. . . .'" Natural processes render all beings uniform, abolish that which differentiates them, and eliminate that which distinguishes them; all this occurs not in order to achieve "structuralist harmony," but rather to create a natural indistinction in which the very idea of difference is stripped of meaning: "any kind of ground will seem good enough to sleep on; you will not see it, as you do now, bristling with thorns, and swarming with insects and infection" (p. 380).

Let me open here a second methodological parenthesis. At every step of the way, structural anthropology seeks relations of opposition and difference: its fundamental postulate is that meaning is provided by the structure. It follows that to meet structuralism's demands for order, the raw material under observation must adhere to rules of combination and permutation. Unfortunately for structural anthropology—and for Lévi-Strauss—nature offers raw material in which one can find neither the possibility of systematization nor the transposition of a model. Any comparison or opposition, however sophisticated, that structuralism might offer us becomes meaningless in the face of the most unforeseen natural juxtapositions, by which the (culturally) signifying phenomena lose their specificity and their meaning. Whether or not the binary oppositions so dear to structuralism have a role to play, the interpenetration of opposite terms and the mixing of genres that are produced by natural indistinction reduce to nothing the separation that is crucial to structural dichotomies. Thus the eagle's speech is essentially an explanation to Augustus of the "confusionist" role played by the sacred—a role that structuralism is not prepared to admit. However, Augustus/Lévi-Strauss immediately recognizes the crux of the issue—he is "made aware of the problem of the relationship between nature and society through his conversation with the eagle" (*ibid.*)—and consequently seeks to resolve this "theoretical" problem with most notable eagerness and promptness.

First, Augustus grasps the fact that the sacred of which the eagle speaks is not something antisocial, but rather a divinity that belongs to the realm of nature: the discourse of the eagle is *antithetical* to society, not antisocial. This is the true source of Augustus's fear: any identification with the divinity would not only be incompatible with his social being, but would also result in his expulsion into nature. His terror intensifies with the appearance of the sacred in the city: "The third act opened in an atmosphere of crisis; on the eve of the ceremony, Rome was swamped by an onrush of the divine: the walls of the imperial palace cracked and it was invaded by plants and animals. The city was returning to the state of nature as if it had been destroyed by a cataclysm" (p. 381). Under these conditions, one can only sympathize with Augustus in his decision to accept, even to choose, assassination by Cinna and thereby gain the *social* immortality to which he aspires, rather than join the gods and find himself turned into a lizard, an insect, or a plant! There follows a complicated assassination plot through which, in the murder of Augustus by Cinna, each will preserve the meaning of his past and gain some form of immortality: "Thus they would both win the immortality they dreamed of: Augustus would enjoy the official immortality of books, statues and worship; and Cinna the black immortality of the regicide, and would thus be reintegrated into society while continuing to oppose it" (p.

380). Nevertheless, all is not yet entirely lost for Augustus, and before he has to fix his choice between the two godly options that confront him (the social and the natural), he makes a final effort to overcome the naturalist problematic through a political solution.

Let me backtrack for a moment and return to the passage that follows the eagle's discourse. The text in its entirety reads as follows: "In the second act, Augustus, having been made aware of the problem of the relationship between nature and society through his conversation with the eagle, decided to see Cinna again; *the latter had in the past preferred nature to society*, the opposite choice to the one which had led Augustus to imperial dignity" (*ibid.*, my emphasis). We detect here a subtle shift in Augustus's thinking. Whereas initially he was against the idea of meeting with Cinna, on further reflection he decides to see his old friend. Moreover, Cinna now stands as the symbol of nature in Augustus's mind. This new symbolic association is confirmed later in the play when, in response to Cinna's description of his foray into nature, Augustus is quick to recognize the eagle's speech:

I [Cinna] have eaten lizards, snakes and grasshoppers; and I approached these foods, the mere thought of which is enough to turn your stomach, with the emotion of one about to be initiated and the conviction that I was going to establish a new link between the universe and myself. . . . [Augustus] recognized with alarm that Cinna was saying the same as the eagle. (p. 381)

Cinna, however, is neither a savage nor a primitive, nor under any circumstances a man from nature, as

Augustus would like us to believe. He is only a social renegade who longs for a return to society, provided that it be on his own terms:

During his ten years of adventure, he had done nothing but think of Camille, the sister of his childhood friend, and whom he could have married had he said the word. Augustus would have been delighted to give her to him. But it would have been intolerable for him to obtain her according to the rules of the social code; he had to win her in defiance of the established order, not through it. Hence his effort to acquire an heretical prestige which would allow him to force society's hand and make it grant him that which it was, in any case, prepared to accord. (p. 380)

The gratuitous aspect of Cinna's challenge shows that, in his case, we are dealing with only a symbolic exigency. And although at times Cinna had been reduced to eating "lizards, snakes and grasshoppers," he nevertheless remains, even at the height of his depression (probably caused by indigestion!), the most social of human beings. In contrast to Lévi-Strauss, who was obsessed with a Chopin melody throughout his stay at Campos Novos, Cinna chooses a more "classical" route: "To fill the emptiness of the endless days I would recite Aeschylus and Sophocles to myself" (*ibid.*). In this respect, Cinna's antisocial character is clearly marked in the text—he rebels against society, against order, and so on—and it is only to emphasize it that the binary opposition of disorder/order keeps surfacing throughout the play.

Yet to reach any resolution of the problem posed by the (sacred) eagle, Augustus must find a "discreet" way to bypass it. Hence—in contrast to Augustus, who represents the social order—Cinna will come to symbolize nature instead of the negation of society. Transposed into the personal register, this shift is best explained as a Lévi-Straussian vision of the world that is totally social and leaves no place, philosophical or methodological, for nature. (It follows that, within such a vision, the opposite of society can never be nature but only that which negates society—for instance, those who violate the interdictions that uphold its order. Thus the purely social and cultural opposition of *disorder/order* is, for Augustus's purposes, usefully substituted for the fundamental *nature/culture* opposition. Ethnological reality is replaced by a structural necessity. For the same reason, it does not take much for Camille to persuade Augustus/Lévi-Strauss "that he had misinterpreted the situation, and that Cinna, rather than the eagle, was the messenger of the gods" (p. 381). Hence Cinna assumes the function of mediator in the unfriendly exchange between the impure eagle and society's representative. And ethnology becomes an affair between the two complementary poles of the social order, which proceed to join forces precisely in order to exclude the intruding eagle: "If this were true, Augustus saw the possibility of a political solution. He had only to trick Cinna for the gods to be deceived at the same time" (*ibid.*).

It is thus by virtue of the intervention of the social misfit, under the guise of a counterfeit nature, that the sacred (the gods) will be taken in hand by the representative of the social order, which had not previously possessed nature. This line of reasoning, by which Augustus is fooling the gods in duping Cinna, is a rationalization intended to conjure away the true representative of nature—namely, the eagle. In view of the resolution of the play, this turn of events provides an interesting commentary. Having disposed of the problem of the eagle, Augustus is no longer anxious to join the ranks of the gods. He thus backs out of his deal with Cinna, without, of course, telling him so:

It was agreed between them that the guards would be withdrawn and then Augustus would offer himself as a defenseless victim to Cinna's dagger. But instead, Augustus secretly arranged for the bodyguard to be doubled so that Cinna did not even get near to him. Confirming the course of their respective careers, Augustus was to succeed in his last undertaking; he would be a god, but a god among men, and he would pardon Cinna. (p. 382)

By such a scheme, Augustus attains a divinity that will spare him both the unpleasantness of impurity and the risks of assassination. Only one piece of the puzzle remains to be solved to properly conclude our reading: we need only substitute, for the foiled murder of Augustus, the symbolic murder of the eagle—and this is, of course, Lévi-Strauss's *necessary* oversight.

Interpreted in this light, the apotheosis of Augustus is fully achieved. Lévi-Strauss need not even provide a conclusion to the imaginary scenario depicted by the play: "I cannot quite remember how it was all supposed to end, as the last scenes remained unfinished" (p. 381).[10] Paradoxically, Lévi-Strauss's forgetfulness stems from an excess of knowledge: he cannot recall the conclusion only because he knows "too much." But in fact the conclusion to the play had been disclosed earlier, albeit offhandedly, by Livia: "The apotheosis was the crowning point of Augustus's career: 'It was exactly what he deserved,' in other words, the Académie Française" (p. 379).

Some thirty years after he imagined Augustus's crowning at the Académie Française, Lévi-Strauss himself was elected to this august body. The interview he subsequently gave to the magazine *Lire* provides a substitute for the missing conclusion of his alter ego's apotheosis:

Interviewer: Is your presence in the Académie a mere anecdote, or does it symbolize your respect for that which lasts throughout the years?

Lévi-Strauss: It is unquestionably the sign of my respect for institutions, for all that endures. I did not try to enter the Académie Française. But when I was asked with insistence, I accepted, for I believe myself to be bound by a sort of duty to participate in the preservation of a value system and of an institution which goes back fairly far into history. . . . I consider the Académie as a historical monument that we should try to preserve.[11]

[10] For a suggestive reading of the non-conclusion of "The Apotheosis," see Jeffrey Mehlman's "Punctuation in *Tristes Tropiques*," in *A Structural Study of Autobiography: Proust, Leiris, Sartre, Lévi-Strauss* (Ithaca, N.Y., 1974), pp. 216–20.

[11] "Entretien avec Lévi-Strauss," in *Lire*, 93 (1983), 106.

The Consequences of Theory

"The study of these savages leads to something other than the revelation of a Utopian state of nature or the discovery of the perfect society in the depths of the forest; it helps us to build a *theoretical model of human society, which does not correspond to any observable reality*" (p. 392, my emphasis). The reader will undoubtedly recognize this passage, in which Lévi-Strauss invokes Rousseau's teachings and which constitutes, in its own terms, structural anthropology's *profession de foi*. It is in this sense that we must understand Lévi-Strauss's oft-repeated claim that structuralism reconciles nature and man under the aegis of structuralist science. Lévi-Strauss must consequently assert at all costs that the structuralist model takes priority over all the relations that it sets up; in other words, he must see not so much a description of the real in the model as a description of the model in the advent of the real. Ultimately, the confrontation with reality (in this case, with nature) becomes impossible, because reality is elided by the model, which serves as reality's only truth. For the model to function, one must eliminate anything that draws attention to the empirical character of facts, especially if those facts belong to "the big book of nature."

Hence Lévi-Strauss refuses to consider relations between nature and culture in any way that is not purely *formal*. It is evidently false to think that the oppositions sought by structural anthropology may not exist in the ethnographic material uncovered by the ethnographer. Such oppositions do, of course, exist, and sometimes play a key structuring role in the constitution of social organization. Nonetheless, it remains true that every aspect of the social life studied by structural anthropology must, in keeping with methodological necessity, eliminate any trace of nature. Thus, for example, the passage from nature to culture is either a *false* problem that this school ignores—only myths deal with this chaotic relation, and no true structuralist science would deign to consider it[12]—or a problem that structuralist anthropology circumvents, by resorting to the ideological and methodological ruse that consists of the kind of metonymic substitution (natural/sacred/impure = antisocial = disorderly) that I have just analyzed.

The imaginary psychodrama provided by "The Apotheosis" is thus produced to dispose of any ethnographic knowledge that would be troublesome for the abstract systematizations on which Lévi-Strauss will found a structuralist theory of culture. What Lévi-Strauss expresses through the voice of the eagle is merely the formulation of a discourse that he is unable to conceptualize, but that he senses to be incompatible with the discourse that he intends to undertake. Hence the eagle is invoked so that the sacred disease that it embodies might be dispelled, and consequently replaced by a healthier structuralist sacred, one assimilated to society. Lévi-Strauss's un-

[12] On this point, see René Girard's *Violence and the Sacred* (Baltimore, Md., 1977), pp. 55–57 and 241–44.

conscious produces the imaginary scenario required
to act as the (laboratory) model that is so necessary to
his general endeavor. Thus as a crucial preliminary
step in approaching empirical reality, Lévi-Strauss
must first live the real according to the modality of the
imaginary, for only in this manner, and in this mode,
can he resolve the theoretical conflict facing ethnological structuralism.

But more generally speaking, what is the link between theoretical knowledge and the knowledge provided by an imaginary production as set out for us by
Lévi-Strauss? In this case, anthropological theory is
made possible only by a willful misprision of the
truth—willful in the sense that Lévi-Strauss obviously knew something all along, yet did not want to
know it. Moreover, let us note that it is a real crisis—
the reconsideration of his vocation—that unleashes
the imaginary scenario that constitutes itself as theory by working through an unbearable recollection.
The memory of the eagle's speech, the memory that
founds and brings about the theory, is unbearable because it involves a murder, albeit one that is symbolic: that of the eagle. Lévi-Strauss conveniently forgets—or rather *must* forget—the eagle's sacrifice in
order to theorize the discourse of structural anthropology. In other words, the truth of the theory mater-
ializes specifically against a backdrop of death: sacrifice or symbolic murder. But in the end who, or
rather what, is really being sacrificed?

Lévi-Strauss's text clearly indicates that theory begins to take shape immediately after the eagle's
speech, that is, at the very moment when Augustus /

Lévi-Strauss is suffering extreme anguish. Freud says that anguish is always anguish in the face of something; in this case, in the face of what? Obviously, Lévi-Strauss feels anguish about the possible return of the particular thing that he does not want to see: the repressed reality. For Lévi-Strauss, anguish is the sign of the imminence of the reality that must be eliminated at all costs, before its irruption onto the scene of his imaginary. In other words, anguish is directly linked to such an unbearable reality that, to protect himself, the individual who must endure it reaches desperately for a figuration—a theory—that allows him to bracket this reality before it overwhelms him. Thus the truth of theory rests upon a founding murder or expulsion, as René Girard would say: not the symbolic murder or expulsion of the eagle but, more fundamentally, that of the real.

What I have tried to argue here is that the passage from personal scenario to theory depends on a fundamental repression of reality. The imaginary fulfills this function by developing scenarios that replace and preempt the real—scenarios that then produce theory by resolving or carrying to another register the antinomies and complications of the real. Hence at the same time that theory claims to stand for the real, the discourse of theory inscribes within itself repression of the very reality that it promotes. This should come as no surprise to any informed reader since, from Proust to Beckett, from Blanchot to Derrida, from Freud to Lacan, and from Lévi-Strauss to Girard, our entire literary and theoretical modernity is predicated on a nostalgia for the real. Either reality is accused of never showing its true face (as in Derrida's concept of *différance*, in which the advent of the real is always deferred) or, when reality does make itself manifest, it falls short of itself (in Lacan's case, the symbolic is the only instance capable of revealing the real; and similarly, for Girard, the reality of desire is always elsewhere, mediated by the desire of a model).

Thus the real, in and of itself, is void, an empty space that gains meaning not from its own manifestation, but always through allusion to an otherness. In Clément Rosset's succinct formulation, "[the real] is the negation of the here to the benefit of the elsewhere."[13] It would be illuminating to pursue a longer study of the tie between theory and this "lack of the real" (our conception of the real as lack), which defines our modernity. But this is not the place for it,[14] although I would like to suggest, however briefly, that the notion of totality, or of closure, that generally accompanies theory is one of the phantasms that serves to satisfy our metaphysical demand for a global and integral hold on the real. As a phantasm of totality, theory covers up the lack of the real that is inscribed at the center of our modernity.

With this in mind, I conclude by recalling a famous

[13] Clément Rosset, "Dénégation de l'ici au profit de l'ailleurs," in *Le Philosophe et les sortilèges* (Paris, 1985), p. 39. Rosset is also quick to diagnose the reason underlying the keen interest evident on the part of contemporary criticism in problems specific to language: one of language's primary traits is that it evokes the real by means of a substitute that is not the real; in other words, language evokes the presence of the real through its absence.

[14] See my *Scenarios of the Imaginary: Theorizing the French Enlightenment* (Ithaca, N.Y., 1987).

Lacanian formula: *Le réel c'est l'impossible.*[15] But for my purposes, I shall transform it into a more appropriate theoretical statement: The real is that which is impossible to grasp, at least in the discourse of theory as we know it today. Theory's incapacity *really* to account for the real or, rather, its inadequation to the demands of the real—therein lies the source of the malaise evident among contemporary theorists who are hypersensitive to this question because, even though they do not attain the real through their theories, the real gets to them, like it or not. *Tristes Théories.* . . .

[15] Jacques Lacan, *Le Séminaire, Livre XI: Les quatre concepts fondamentaux de la psychanalyse* (Paris, 1973), p. 152; see also p. 253.

Film Theory and the Two Imaginaries

Thomas M. Kavanagh

> Never did any of all this amount to a real vision. It
> was always only the illusion of one, as if it were
> only the vision of his visions. . . . It was always as if
> a picture had just flashed across the mysterious
> screen, and he never succeeded in catching hold of
> it. There was all the time a restlessness and uneasi-
> ness in him such as one feels when watching
> cinematographic pictures.
>
> Robert Musil, *Young Törless*

> Je pense où je ne suis pas par la pensée, donc je suis
> où je ne pense pas.
>
> Jacques Lacan, *Ecrits*

The above passage from *Young Törless* certainly qualifies that novel of 1906 as one of the first literary works to use the then new experience of film spectatorship as a metaphor of our epistemological relationship to what is seen but unknown. From its inception, film has tantalized its viewers with the acutely dubious pleasure of seeing what would otherwise be unseen, yet at the same time provoking profound doubts as to their real grasp of the vision so provided. As Musil's text eloquently indicates, film quickly became a metaphor for the impossible enterprise of trying to understand that by which we are fascinated.

Only eleven years after Lumière first used the darkened theater on the rue de Rennes to show small Parisian audiences his images of a train entering the Ciotat station, we find a European writer in another country referring to this new form of visual representation not in terms of its Muybridgean promise of something that will expand and consolidate our knowledge of the world around us, but as an emblem of illusion. Film, Musil seems to be saying, offers its spectator an experience of frustration and inadequacy comparable to the intersubjective dialectic of capture and evasion that distorts our every attempt to know that which we desire. To watch a fascinating other leads, as does the film projected on a screen before us, not to an understanding of that other, but to profound and troubling doubts about our ability ever to behold that fascinating other outside the distortions of our scrutiny.

Musil's metaphor is important because it points to an aspect of film viewing that has been consistently repressed in every attempt to constitute an adequate theory—or, for that matter, even an adequate history—of film. Musil's doubts as to the suitability of spectatorship as a basis for knowledge can also be read as emblematic of the much larger question of the status of theory in general, as an enterprise claiming both to preserve and to dominate the given of our perception. Musil invites us to consider the question of

what film, the most important representational art
form of the twentieth century, might tell us about the
structure, foundation, and limits of our desire to theorize.

On the most obvious level, the study of film as an
object of scholarly reflection, and even more so as an
academic discipline, is everywhere marked by the absence of any single, generally accepted definition of
its object. Anyone working in the field quickly discovers that nothing approaching a canon of great, significant, or axial works can be pointed to as a sufficient corpus whose study and understanding are assumed to ensure a command of the medium's history,
structure, forms, or function.

Lists do exist. But, for the most part, they are the
result of one or another arguably extraneous and always partial grid having been imposed on cinema as
a whole. A history of film as a technology of representation would isolate certain works as important
because they played a pioneering role in introducing
or exploiting innovations in ocular physics, emulsion
chemistry, or sound-recording techniques. A history
of film genres would look to the rise and fall, as well
as to the transformational resuscitations, of certain
prototypical configurations of represented milieus,
thematic clusters, and diegetic patterns. Or, yielding
to the ever-lingering temptation to borrow from traditional literary studies, we might have instead a history of the great directors: the *auteurs*, those individual creative geniuses recognized as key figures in the
medium's development.

These are, of course, only three possibilities drawn from the much larger number of possible "histories of cinema" we might imagine. It was as a reaction against both the inadequacy of any such approach and the inevitable eclecticism, theoretical as well as practical, of attempting to combine them that, in the mid-1960's, led Christian Metz to develop the first scientific model for film study as that of a form without a history, a methodology without a canon. Metz rarely talks about particular films. Nowhere in his works do we find the beginnings of a pantheon of great works or great directors. Jacques Rosier's *Adieu Philippine*, for instance, is one of the few films discussed at length in the first volume of *Essais sur la signification au cinéma*.[1] This film is chosen, however, not because it is technologically innovative, central to the development of a particular genre, or the work of a great director. Rosier's admittedly minor work is chosen because everything that is specific about it readily evaporates into a properly theoretic vision of *la grande syntagmatique*: a series of formal structures that are important precisely because, as Metz would have it, they can be shown to function as the semiotic armatures of all narrative film.

This first semiology of film was, quite resolutely and quite self-consciously, a theory of the text. Individual films were approached as plethoras of signifying codes—codes of the image, sound codes, diegetic codes, and so forth—which interact within the

[1] Christian Metz, *Film Language: A Semiotics of the Cinema* (New York, 1974), provides a partial translation of the studies in this volume.

greater whole of the filmic text. This first semiology, the semiology of the film as text, borrowed its analytic tools from linguistics—linguistics not, despite the naïve criticism so often made of Metz's first books, as a theoretical parti pris somehow impoverishing the hypothetical richness of the image, but linguistics as the first discipline to be marked by the development of a series of concepts allowing the critic to arrive at a truly semiotic understanding of the filmic signifier.

During the last ten years, this exclusive preoccupation with the film as text, with the explicit formalism of a basically linguistic model, has been redefined by what is now referred to as the "second semiology," the semiology of film most coherently set forth in Metz's key text, *Le Signifiant imaginaire*.[2] In its broadest implications this second semiology represents a displacement of critical inquiry away from the film as artifact, the film as a system of self-defining codic elaborations, to the space between film and spectator, to the process of film viewing as an ongoing dialectic between spectator and spectacle. Turning its attention away from purely conscious, secondary processes and their analysis through linguistic models, this second semiology seeks to understand the shape of the primary processes that are at work in the spectatorial psyche as it encounters the filmic object. Its

[2] Christian Metz, *The Imaginary Signifier: Psychoanalysis and Cinema* (Bloomington, Ind., 1982). All quotations are from the English translation.

elected tools are, for the most part, concepts borrowed from psychoanalysis, more specifically from Lacan's reading of Freud.

In one sense, this displacement of text by spectator is an attempt to come to grips with a question that was all but totally neglected in the first semiology. Metz and his disciples, as they extended their attempts to consolidate what might be described as an impersonal phenomenology of the filmic text, found themselves more and more preoccupied by another question, a question they came to recognize as primordial to any attempt to understand cinema as an institution: Why do we go to the movies? Why do we do so with such pleasure and so frequently that satisfying that desire has led to the creation of an industry whose economic and cultural impact is one of the principal factors to be considered in any analysis of contemporary Western society?

In defining this second semiology, Metz and his followers found themselves working more closely than had ever been the case with literary studies at the interface of desire and theory, of pleasure and a need to dominate that pleasure through understanding. This new theory of film embodied in the second semiology confronted the reality of the spectator's desire not only as the basis of his relation to the pleasurable object, but as the motivating force behind their own decision to theorize about such desire.

The pleasure of film viewing has, since the inception of the medium, been felt to be grounded in the spectator's heightened participation in an "imaginary" dimension made particularly accessible by film. Edgar Morin, in what was perhaps the most extreme statement of this position, argued as early as 1958 for an almost anthropological redefinition of human experience through its mediation by cinematic representation.[3] Metz points out in *Le Signifiant imaginaire* that the word "imaginary" as it applies to an understanding of film must be taken both in the everyday sense of the word as designating something that is unreal (since the vast majority of films are fictional narratives speaking to us of purely imagined worlds) and, more importantly, in the Lacanian sense whereby the imaginary designates that dimension of our experience rooted in the bliss of the child's immediate, undeferred relation to the mother. The imaginary in this more specialized sense holds the promise of a simulated return to a time before the structuring of our consciousness by the œdipal conflict, a time before our forced integration into the realm of law and mediation that Lacan refers to as the symbolic. Our susceptibility to the pleasure of the imaginary is, for Lacan, the enduring mark of the mirror stage as both a discovery and an alienation of the self within the beholding of its reflected image. The imaginary determines our quest for selfhood as an impossible striving to become the double of that reflected image in which we first perceive our wholeness.

From Jean Epstein's and Luis Buñuel's descriptions

[3] Edgar Morin, *Le Cinéma ou l'homme imaginaire* (Paris, 1958).

of cinema as a kind of waking dream[4] to contemporary analyses of spectatorship as a literal reenactment of Lacan's mirror stage, the pleasure of watching a film has been approached as an experience situated outside the demands of the symbolic and offering the spectator the temporary yet privileged illusion of coincidence with a pre-œdipal experience of the imaginary. Since the imaginary has, for the viewing subject, subsequently been relegated to the unconscious, attempts to describe its role in film spectatorship have most often adopted the Freudian economic model, according to which the pleasure of film viewing results from a return of the repressed in a form sufficiently modified to disarm the censoring agency of the superego: "If," Metz claims, "a subject is to 'like' a film, the detail of the diegesis must sufficiently please his conscious and unconscious phantasies to permit him a certain instinctual satisfaction, and this satisfaction must stay within certain limits, must not pass the point at which anxiety and rejection would be mobilised" (*The Imaginary Signifier*, p. 111).

One result of this approach has been a sometimes oversimplified emphasis on the film's content and characters as vehicles of the spectator's subconscious identification. Liliana Cavani's *Night Porter*, for example, would be, for those so disposed, a particularly fascinating film because its characters and situations

[4] See the posthumous collection of Epstein's writings published under the title *Esprit du cinéma* (Paris, 1955). For Buñuel's most concise statement of this position, see the text of his address delivered at the University of Mexico in 1953, "Poetry and Cinema," reprinted in *Luis Buñuel* by Ado Kyrou (New York, 1963), pp. 108–12.

allow the spectator's otherwise repressed sadoma-sochism to discover itself in this lurid, autumnal tale of a dispossessed SS doctor who reenters a lover's paradise at the beckoning of his concentration camp victim-become-mistress.

In his key article, "Effects idéologiques de l'appareil de base,"[5] Jean-Louis Baudry opened up a new dimension in our understanding of the role of the imaginary within film viewing. Through an analysis of the *form* of filmic representation—the fact, for instance, that montages, zooms, and other special effects posit the spectator's consciousness as existing beyond all restraints of real time and space—he has shown that, whatever the film's explicit content, all narrative cinema offers the spectator an imaginary identification with the film's distinctly "unreal" sequence of images and sounds. The film itself, as a form, offers the illusion of a transcendental ego, of a sense of self that, amid the formless welter of perception, confirms its transcendence through the unity and coherence characterizing the ideational synthesis of meaning presented by the film:

The spectator identifies less with what is represented, the spectacle itself, than with what sets the spectacle in play, puts it on stage. He identifies with what itself is invisible but which makes something be seen; makes it be seen in the same movement as he, the spectator, sees. Obliging the spectator to see what he sees is the function assigned to the

[5] This article, originally published in *Cinéthique*, no. 7/8 (1970), has been included in *L'Effet cinéma* (Paris, 1978), along with Baudry's later article "Le Dispositif" and a number of interviews with filmmakers.

camera as relay. Just as the mirror reassembles the fragmented body within the ego's imaginary reintegration, this transcendental ego brings together the discontinuous fragments of phenomena, of the lived, within a reunifying meaning. Through it, each element takes on meaning by integrating itself within an "organic" unit. Between the imaginary assumption of the fragmented body into unity and the transcendence of the ego providing an integrative meaning, the flow is indefinitely reversible. (p. 25)

In his later article "Le Dispositif," Baudry carries his argument a step farther in claiming that the fundamental drive at work throughout the history of cinema's development has been that of "constructing a simulation machine capable of offering the viewing subject perceptions that have all the characteristics of representations taken for perceptions" (p. 47). This definition is important because it allows Baudry to argue for a scientific basis to what was long perceived as a similarity of function between cinema and the dream. The dreamwork, as Freud analyzed it, is likewise one in which representations—psychic representations generated by the interaction of the conscious, preconscious, and unconscious—are, for as long as the dream lasts, taken by the dreamer as reality, as actual perceptions. Watching a film can then be seen as accomplishing the same function as the dream to the extent that the film—bits and pieces of image and sound—is perceived as forming a coherent whole endowed with signification. For Baudry, the only important difference between dream and cinema comes from the fact that, in a dream, the subject experiences only the stimulation of his own psyche, whereas the film viewer depends on images and sounds coming from an independent agency, the film itself. Alone in a darkened room, cut off from the outside world, fixed in a state of minimal bodily activity, the spectator undergoes passively the same mental processes that, in dreams and hallucinations, he actively initiates as a form of psychic gratification.

Baudry's conclusion is not that cinema is a dream, but rather that "cinema reproduces an impression of reality; it initiates a *cinema-effect* that is comparable to the impression of the *reality-effect* caused by the dream. The entire cinematographic apparatus is aimed at provoking this simulation: it is indeed, then, the simulation of a particular state of the subject, a *subject-effect* and not a *reality-effect*" (p. 48).

In a text written a quarter of a century earlier, Octave Mannoni, discussing the role of the imaginary in theater, isolated an implicit tendency within theatrical representation that, according to Baudry's analysis, finds its most complete form only in the psychic state of the film viewer:

When the curtain goes up, the imaginary powers of the ego are both liberated and organized, dominated, by the spectacle. It is difficult to express this idea since, metaphorically, the word "stage" [*scène*] has itself been adopted as the term designating that place within the psyche where our images parade. . . . The theatrical stage becomes the extension of the ego in all its imaginary potentialities. . . . If someone, an actor, shows us that a particular role can be assumed, he is at the same time revealing something else

to us: the very possibility of playing a role, our whole reserve of imaginary roles, all the lives that we do not live, all
the remedies for boredom.[6]

The desire that brings us to the cinema, the pleasure
of film viewing, is thus presented as intimately
linked to this promised apotheosis of the ego, of the
self as an imaginary construct determining yet re-
sisting all its only partial integrations within a sanctioned and always alienated identity imposed by the
dictates of the law and the symbolic.

Perhaps the most radical reflection on the all-powerful rule of the spectator's imaginary within the process of film viewing can be found in Hans Jürgen Syberberg's *Hitler ein Film aus Deutschland*. By its very
title, which lacks a semicolon or comma between
Hitler and *A Film from Germany*, this work cautions
us not to look at its seven hours of images and sounds
as simply a film *about* Hitler. It is, rather, an extended
meditation on the premise that Hitler—both as an individual object of collective fantasy and as a sum-
marizing eponym of Nazism—might be best understood as a kind of absolute, society-wide *film* through
which a particular imaginary of the German public
chose to identify, liberate, and consume itself in a single mythic figure incarnating the full force and
twisted contours of Germany's post-romantic, post-
Diktat, post-inflationary agony. With an astounding
daring, this film invites us to reverse our usual understanding of the relation between ideological su-

[6] Octave Mannoni, "L'Illusion comique," in *Clefs pour l'imaginaire ou
l'autre scène* (Paris, 1969), pp. 181–82.

perstructure and economic infrastructure. What if, Syberberg seems to ask, the specific imaginary of Nazism were no longer to be dismissed as a baroque obfuscation of more fundamental economic and social realities? What if those "realities" were seen only as minor caveats infinitely pliable to the contortions of a society-wide imaginary insisting that, at any price, the film must go on? What we are watching, Syberberg tells us, is not a disaster film, but the film as disaster.

Pushed to its extreme, Syberberg's film can, by the ambitiousness of its intent, be seen as raising a central question about our understanding of film viewing. What if, rather than looking to the metapsychology of the solitary dreamer, we were to look instead to the mass hypnosis of such rituals as the Nuremberg rallies for a possible explanation of the spectator's pleasure? Explicitly organized as "cathedrals of light," those collective spectacles set out to induce an entranced, unreal effect on their spectators/participants that was everywhere orchestrated toward a phantasmagorical redefinition, each by the others, of a manipulated reality, an implicit ideal, and a mass dream: precisely the three elements that, in a quite different context, Metz points to as comprising what he calls *la visée filmique*, filmic intent.

In posing his question this way—in asking who, finally, is *in control* of what is perceived and how it is perceived—Syberberg comes close to what has been one of the most important results of film theory's "second semiology." The analysis of film spectatorship made possible by the massive importation of psychoanalytic concepts has led to an acute awareness of the necessarily problematic status of our own discourse as would-be theorists of film. Facing this difficulty head-on, Metz begins *Le Signifiant imaginaire* with the following definition: "Film theory . . . is an attempt to disengage the cinema-object from the imaginary and to win it for the symbolic in the hope of extending the latter by a new province. It is an enterprise of displacement, a territorial enterprise, a symbolizing advance" (p. 3).

The problem Metz addresses here is as simple as it is inevitable. As theorist, his task is to arrive at an understanding of film that, because it is elaborated from a distance, can control and analyze objectively the encounter with the imaginary that he sees as central to all film viewing. As a spectator who chooses to watch a film, he is taken up by the pleasure it offers, manipulated both by its and by his own illusions. Yet his intention to theorize about film and its effects on the spectator implies that his theoretical discourse somehow elaborates itself beyond such manipulation. As a film viewer who goes on to write about the films viewed, he finds himself, vis-à-vis the force of the imaginary, in a position similar to that described by Mannoni in his discussion of the stage technician. In relation to the play he oversees, this stage technician is defined by a necessarily ironic distance from the spectacle as spectacle. Unlike all the happily inebriated theatergoers around him, he must approach that spectacle as a connoisseur, as someone who never actually consumes, as "a wine taster who spits out the wine and never swallows" (p. 162).

The ideal mental state for the would-be film theorist becomes, as Metz describes it, a kind of benevolent schizophrenia:

I have loved the cinema. I no longer love it. I still love it. . . . Trying to construct the film into an object of knowledge is to extend, by a supplementary degree of sublimation, the passion for seeing which made both the cinephile and the institution themselves. Initially an undivided passion entirely occupied in preserving the cinema as a good object (an imaginary passion, a passion for the imaginary), it subsequently splits into two diverging and reconverging desires, one of which "looks" at the other: this is the theoretical break; and, like all breaks, it is also a link: the link of theory with its object. (p. 79)

According to Metz, this "break" will ultimately serve to forge an even stronger link to the object about which the theorist would speak. But the question that Metz's formulation leaves unanswered and finally obfuscates is that of what other imaginary dimension, what other allegiance, is called into play by the would-be theorist as he carries out his programmatic task of displacing what he has experienced as pleasure into the symbolic registers of knowledge and theory.

In a work first published in 1978, the text of his 1954–55 seminar on the function of the self in Freud's theory and in psychoanalytic technique,[7] Lacan presents an analysis of the self that is particularly pertinent to this question of *le moi du théoricien*, of the theorist as someone functioning at this nexus of the

[7]Jacques Lacan, *Le Seminaire II: le moi dans la théorie de Freud et dans la technique de la psychanalyse* (Paris, 1978).

imaginary and the symbolic. Rather than approaching this question of the self through the tripartite division at the core of Freud's metapsychology (the ego, the id, and the superego), Lacan insists that "the self, in its most essential aspect, is a function of the imaginary. . . . The central, fundamental structure of all experience is specifically of the imaginary order" (p. 50). Grounding his definition of the self within the same imaginary order that plays so crucial a role in the pleasure of film viewing, Lacan's statement has important implications for the Metzian claim that theory might define itself as displacement *from* the imaginary *to* the symbolic.

Throughout this work, Lacan insists that it is within the imaginary, and according to its structures, that the self establishes its relations to the objects around it. Approaching the self-object relation from this perspective, Lacan insists not only that the self's relation to the object is always a form of desire, but that this same imaginary dimension remains an integral part even of that self-distancing desire we see as generating knowledge and *savoir*—the objectified domain in which the theorist would situate his own particular discourse. The value of Lacan's position, of his insistence that the desiring self and the imaginary be seen as the pertinent context for all knowledge, becomes clear when we realize that, understood in this way, knowledge, like all object relations, ultimately reveals itself as a form of narcissism: "In order that there be any relation to the object, there must already exist a narcissistic relation of the self to that other.

This is, in fact, the primordial condition of all objectivization of the outside world—and it is equally true of scientific objectivizations as of their naïve, spontaneous variants" (p. 118).

Interestingly enough, particularly as concerns our own question of the relation between the film spectator and the film theorist, Lacan claims that it is the eye, the seat of all scopophilic desire, that is most fundamental to narcissism: "Our task is to understand which organs are involved in this narcissistic, imaginary relation to the other through which the self elaborates, *bildet*, itself. The imaginary structuring of the self takes place around the specular image of the specific body, the image of the other. And the relation of looking to the thing looked at is the province of one organ, the eye, to call it by its name" (p. 119).

This importance accorded to the visual brings us back to Lacan's notion of the mirror stage and the long debate in film theory as to its value as a model for understanding film spectatorship. Metz, for instance, although expressing some misgivings about Baudry's massive appeal to the mirror stage as a paradigm for all film viewing, nonetheless accepts its importance on the condition that, as concerns film viewing, it be understood that we are dealing with "a mirror without a tain": a "transparent" mirror in which the specific, physical body of the spectator can never be among the objects reflected. Despite the apparent aptness of Metz's proviso, we should not proceed to a summary dismissal of what is really at stake in Lacan's insistence that it is the mirror stage that provides the enduring form to all subsequent object relations:

What have I tried to make understood by the mirror stage? That what is disconnected, in pieces, anarchic in man establishes its relation to his perception on the level of a completely original tension. It is the image of his own body that provides the principle for all unity that he will perceive in objects. And, by reason of that image, he will always perceive unity prematurely and as something outside of himself. Because of this double relation to himself, the objects within his world will find their structure within the wandering shadow of his own self. These objects will all have a status that is fundamentally anthropomorphic, even, we might say, egomorphic. (p. 198)

In explaining the importance of the mirror stage, Lacan introduces a second metaphor that is particularly relevant to the problem of the film theorist. Specifically, Lacan attempts to represent within a single image what he sees as a dialectic that is initiated in the mirror stage but that endures as an ongoing structure of all human experience. The dialectic in question here is that between the perceiving self and the immediacy of sensation, between the self as an instance of knowledge and the apparently unmediated and apodictic status of those data impinging upon the senses. Lacan's intent is to illustrate why the perceiving self cannot be accepted as a *unity* of consciousness, as a sovereign agency of awareness similar to the Cartesian dream of a subjectivity opening itself to stimuli situated outside and independent of itself. On the contrary, he insists, the perceiving self must be seen as one element *within* this dialectic with its sensations. Rather than sovereign master, the self is that against which sensation is always in a state of dialectical tension and mutual redefinition.

The metaphor Lacan proposes, one I would suggest as emblematic of the filmic spectator in his attempts to function as theorist, is an image drawn from fifteenth-century iconography: that of a blind man carrying on his shoulders a sighted paralytic. For Lacan, the seeing paralytic, considered prior to his being lifted up and put in motion by the blind man, represents the limit of subjectivity, the illusion of subjectivity, the only potential subjectivity of a time before its organization through the experience of the mirror stage. Frozen in immobility, the lone paralytic is incapable of designating any self independent of the sensations it perceives but over which it exercises no control. Only when he is carried by the blind man can the paralytic, now caught up in the illusion of a movement ratifying his claim to an independent subjectivity, pretend to his status as one who knows.

The lesson within this metaphor, as Lacan would have it, lies in the way this illusory image of the self as unified subject can never exist outside its dialectical identification with the blind man who supplements his paralysis and immobility. The paralytic may well see; but the diacritical differentiations defining the core of his vision could neither have been initiated nor continue independently of the blind man on whose shoulders he is perched.

Applying this figure to the question of the film theorist and the status of his critical discourse, we might understand the paralytic as the member of the pair endowed with the particular sight of theory. The blind man, on the other hand, might be understood as the member of the pair limited to the immediate fascination of sensation, a consciousness incapable of achieving the crucial distance of the theorist but nonetheless essential to that ongoing dialectic of perception and representation of which he is an integral part. Just as the sighted paralytic is the agency of theory, so the blind man is an emblem of that essentially imaginary dimension of spectatorship everywhere determining the subject's experience of that which he beholds.

Insisting that this relation of paralytic to blind man must itself be seen as a version of the master-slave dialectic, Lacan's analysis allows us to understand that the theorist's fundamental pretense is to an identical mystified ability to operate outside of, independently of, and without interference from the imaginary—that essential dimension of the viewer's pleasure that the theorist hypothesizes away as the purely vehicular support to his own, more noble sight.

The point of Lacan's argument is that the blind man, the support, always continues to operate within those visions the paralytic might perceive and pretend to dominate. The blind man, expelled from the theoretic endeavor, represents that sightless self at the core of every vision beheld by the paralytic:

that which masters the paralytic [our theorist] is the image of the self, which is blind, and which carries him. Contrary to all appearances, and this is the whole problem of the dialectic, it is not, as Plato would have it, the master who mounts the horse, that is to say, the slave. It is the opposite. And the seeing paralytic, the point from which this perspective is constructed, can only identify with his unity in fascination, in the fundamental immobility by which he comes to correspond with the look in which he is captured, the blind look. (p. 66)

Pushed to its most radical implications, Lacan's analysis of knowledge as but one form of an ultimately narcissistic desire would seem to imply that film theory, the displacement into the symbolic of what the film spectator experiences within the imaginary, is impossible. The theorist's fundamental pretension to the sight of theory, the Greek *theōrein*, as a contemplation and control through critical perspectivism, reveals itself to be a mystified, narcissistic claim to operate independently of the imaginary. To face this dilemma directly—to recognize film theory as, at least in its more grandiose pretensions, an inevitably utopian voyage—is to open ourselves to an understanding of what I would call the second imaginary of film theory.

As a spectator viewing a film, I am, to the extent that I take pleasure in it and I am fascinated by it, participating in a dimension of my imaginary evoked and prolonged by the film as object. But to the extent that I go on to represent that experience within a properly symbolic discourse, I do so through calling into play and appealing to a second allegiance, a second imaginary identification. Here, however, my identification is not with the film as object but with my own status as theorist, with myself as he who would be recognized by others as the instance of an adequate and valid symbolic discourse on the films of which I speak.

What first appears as an impossibility of the imaginary's displacement into the symbolic, the Metzian definition of film theory, finds its solution within a dialectic of imaginaries, a balancing of imaginary against imaginary. Rich with my pleasure as spectator, I insist that that pleasure become the material and support of a second, apparently symbolizing movement whereby what is consolidated is my identification with a second narcissistic imaginary: that of my status as theorist, as a double of He Who Knows.

Taken up by the film's fascination, spectator enamoured of the spectacle, I am able to achieve the distance through which my vision will elaborate itself as theory only by reason of this second, equally imaginary identification. Rather than being "taken in" by the spectacle, I must, as theorist, move outside it and look at it as someone no longer caught within it.

This second imaginary of the self as theorist is, of course, relevant to all endeavors that attempt to situate themselves within an exclusively symbolizing dimension. The specific example of film theory is, however, particularly revealing because few other bodies of knowledge take as their object of study an experience that is so radically situated within the pleasures of the imaginary. It is perhaps for this reason that the history of film theory—its schools and chap-

els, its revered masters and faithful disciples, their reciprocal disdain and preening intolerance—reveals so
clearly the felicities and dangers of this second imaginary.

My transformation from pleasured spectator to
knowing theorist—because it is the function of a dou-
bly imaginary identification, because it seeks an ultimately impossible replication of the other within
the self—easily falls prey to a particularly debilitating exacerbation. According to a movement common
to all forms of paranoia, to all threatened losses of the
sanctioning other with which I would identify, the allegiance to this second imaginary of the self as theorist can only be achieved through the refusal to recognize within my discourse any trace of that first, un-
controlled, spectatorial imaginary that I share with
even the most naïve viewer. This enforced repression
of the imaginary roots of my experience as film
viewer most often takes the form of an excessive, if
not exclusive, psychic investment in the quest for absolute congruence with that single other who can
guarantee my status as theorist: the other as Master
and as Master Theorist, whose doubling within myself becomes the single goal my discourse sets out to
achieve.

It is the primacy of this goal of congruence with the
Master that accounts for what is perhaps the most dis-
tressing aspect of so much contemporary film theory:
its elaboration through a dialectic of mimetic rivalry
focused all but exclusively on the pronouncements of
the perceived Master. In one of the most stimulating

of the recent books on film, George Wilson eloquently describes the results of this tendency:

Too often in recent film theory one discovers lengthy and extremely abstract disquisitions on, for example, the relation of film to reality, the languagelike character of film presentation, whose Platonic purity is almost totally unsullied by illustration or evidence. These lofty theoretical edifices rise so grandly over the plain upon which the disorderly mass of actual films is strewn that it is often obscure just what issues are being addressed and how the results of so much theory-building labor are connected with anything one cares about in film.[8]

Many of the most bristlingly doctrinaire, aridly repetitive, and sadly predictable pronouncements marking the history of film theory might more profitably be analyzed not within the context of their supposed object—an understanding of film—but as singularly convoluted forms of this mimetic rivalry linking disciple to master within the theoretic enterprise.

In his two major works, *Dire Mastery* and *Psychoanalysis Never Lets Go*,[9] François Roustang has presented what is perhaps the most convincing study of this impossible imitation of the sanctioning master. While centering his analysis on the particularly intense sadomasochistic relations that Freud as master theorist established with such disciples as Abraham, Jung, Tausk, and Groddeck, Roustang nonetheless

[8] George Wilson, *Narration in Light* (Baltimore, Md., 1986), p. 12.
[9] François Roustang, *Dire Mastery* and *Psychoanalysis Never Lets Go* (Baltimore, Md., 1982 and 1984). All quotations are from these English editions.

isolates an aspect of this phenomenon that is entirely relevant to our question of the film theorist and his potentially debilitating allegiance to the second imaginary of his identification with the master.

Posing the key question of why anyone should choose to become a disciple, Roustang points out that it is done, quite simply, to avoid going mad. No one, as a superficial moralism might have it, becomes a disciple out of laziness. On the contrary, the disciple's fate is one of endless work and eternal vigilance. He accepts the impossible task of attempting first to understand and then to justify and reproduce a discourse whose organizing principle is, by definition, situated outside himself in the unattainable mind of the master.

We become disciples to avoid going mad in the sense that, as disciples, we escape the threat that our theoretical discourse be labeled pure delirium. The master-disciple relationship, and it alone, can draw a firm line of demarcation between theory and delirium: "Delirium is the theory of the *one*, while theory is the delirium of several, which is transmissible. My disciples, who remember my words and propagate them, release me from my solitary speech, and transform it into science and a principle of communication" (*Mastery*, p. 34).

Facing directly a threat lurking at the confines of all scientific endeavors, Roustang goes on to isolate in a particularly provocative way the danger of repudiation that discipleship always carries with it. As disciples defined by the intensity of our libidinal investment in an absolute identification with the master, we run the risk of losing, of cutting ourselves off from all contact with our own experience, with the pleasures and discoveries of our prior status as spectators whose fantasies and imaginaries are as yet undetermined by the master's mediation:

To submit ourselves to the already elaborated theory of another by making it our own, by trying to speak that theory, is to force our fantasizing into the mold of a rationality or rationalization which corresponds not to our own fantasies and desires, but to those of the other. This not only means that our own fantasizing is refused and repressed; but, even more radically, that we have chosen to ignore the fact that the other's theory is itself founded on his fantasizing. . . . We end up not only repressing fantasies and desires, but eliminating all recognition of the importance of such fantasizing or, in the broad sense, of delirium to theory. We find ourselves in the position of the repudiated subject, a condition necessary for scientific thought, but one which is inimical to any adequate theory. (p. 57)

One might, of course, object that Roustang is speaking here of psychoanalytic theory, and that its need to maintain contact with the unconscious need not find a parallel in the domain of film theory. To the extent, however, that we recognize film as a medium always speaking to and through the spectatorial unconscious and its elaboration within the imaginary, the film theorist finds himself operating under quite similar obligations and risks to the unconscious experience of his imaginary as spectator.

The lesson Roustang's analysis might teach us is

not that the place of the master must be vacated, that film theory as a symbolizing discourse should elaborate itself as an unmediated adherence to its object as presence. It is, on the contrary, that as theorists we must accept our position at the nexus, at the point of intersection and disfigurement, between two different levels of the imaginary. Our goal as theorists—as the inevitable subjects of what I have called the second imaginary—must not be to lose ourselves in a hopeless quest for identity with the master.

Film theory can preserve its contact with the object about which it would speak only if it recognizes its discourse as one alternating between, yet never choosing between, two imaginaries, each of which depends intimately and ultimately on the other. Rather than accepting the Metzian imperative calling for a displacement from the imaginary to the symbolic, the theorist must set himself the perhaps less imperial but far more realistic goal of extending and prolonging a pleasure whose fascination theory seeks both to comprehend and to communicate.

The enterprise of film theory, understood as an activity situated between these two imaginaries, becomes prototypical of what is in fact the only possible critical response to the modernist work of art. Eschewing any validation through its conformity to an established canon, the modernist work explicitly sets out to impose and justify itself through an aesthetics rooted in a dimension of the spectator's response that it recognizes as eminently idiosyncratic, as part of a subjectivity that the modernist work itself will fashion and reveal. My pleasure as a spectator is seen as depending on that momentary but enthralling access that the work of art offers to what I do not yet know, to an unconscious dimension of my psyche that emerges into consciousness only incompletely and as a continuation of the artist's work.

The role of the theorist confronted with such an aesthetics becomes one not of mastery and demonstration, but of continuing and turning back upon itself that process of questioning initiated and continued by the spectator's actual experience of the work.

The best film criticism, either as analyses of specific works or as more abstract considerations of formal structures, strives to maintain and extend a process of interrogation, a calling into question of our certainties, which flows directly from our experience of the filmic work itself. The only alternative to the dismal choice between the narcissism of a total surrender to our spectatorial imaginary and an impossible quest for identity with the Master lies in the critic's commitment to prolonging the scope and resonance of those questions posed by the film itself. Rather than allowing our critical discourse to be dominated by the dictates of any "correct theory," it is to the always problematic substance of the film itself as an evolving field of visible significance that we must return. Only in so doing, only in continuing and explicating the film's implicit questions of the perceptions it offers, can theory respect its limits as a discourse whose ultimate obligation is to maintain contact with those interrogations opened up by the film itself.

Toward a Sociology of Theory

Theory and Its Terrors

René Girard

Writing about literary criticism is not something I do very often. It is difficult not to offend some people when you speak about criticism. In a short text, I cannot mention every trend, and I may well offend the trends I will mention even more than the trends I will not. It is impossible not to be a little polemical on such a subject. Let me be polemical right from the start and proclaim that I am polemical openly and explicitly instead of deviously and underhandedly, as is often the fashion nowadays.

You should take what I say with a grain of salt. I am not really as one-sided as I will seem, but to make at least a few points one must inevitably be a little schematic and one-sided. Everything I say can also be turned against me, and you are welcome to play the game if you enjoy it.

Most of us here belong to departments of modern literature. We take the existence of these departments for granted, but in the life of universities they do not go back very far; they are relatively recent creations.

The Middle Ages had nothing of the sort. As in the

ancient world, rhetoric was taught, but not "literature" as we understand it. Fiction was generally regarded as mediocre escapism, and it shared in the general contempt of the learned for whatever was written
in the vulgar dialects, the forerunner of the national
European languages. The only language of culture
was Latin.

At the time of the Renaissance, interest in classical
culture became intense. The humanists studied and
edited Greek and Roman texts. Greek and Latin literature became a legitimate object of study.

This was not true of "literature" in our sense. It was
too lively and productive to become an academic subject. It was left to the creative writers themselves and
to their readers.

Departments of literature were created rather late
in the nineteenth century, at a time when the study
of ancient culture was on the decline. As the role of
Greek and Latin shrank in the education of gentle-
men, the role of the modern national literatures increased. Another factor was romanticism and the rise
of European nationalism. In each country, the national literature became a national heritage, the preservation and cultivation of which was entrusted to
the professors of literature, just as the aesthetic heritage was entrusted to museum curators.

With nationalism on the rise, history, and especially the national history of each country, became
the dominant discipline of the humanities, and literary studies were first conceived as adjuncts to the
study of that national history. Until World War II, the
professors of literature who dedicated their careers

either to critical editions or to literary history were in the majority. "Criticism" or "literary interpretation" in our sense did not exist.

The literary historians and the authors of critical editions were greatly influenced by the positivistic and scientistic temper of the time. They came under the sway of the greatest cultural force of the modern centuries, which is the secularization of intelligence, the decline of religion.

The force that was supposed to displace religion was science, and whatever passed for science at any given moment was embraced with blind passion. The historians of literature fancied themselves scientists dispelling the myths of sacred origins. The sun of objective knowledge was dissolving the fogs of an obscurantist past, replacing poetic legends and transcendental nonsense with the hard facts of the national and bourgeois struggle for a place in the sun.

In the early twentieth century, these positivistic professors of literature remained impervious to the living literature of the time, which was turning against positivism. As early as romanticism, of course, artists and writers had felt uncomfortable with scientism. The early manifestations of the modern industrial and bureaucratic society were uncongenial to most "intellectuals."

To those whose aspirations were not satisfied by the matter-of-fact world in which they lived, the teaching of literature in universities appeared to be a kind of haven. Inevitably, a more romantic, intuitive, and irrational trend began to challenge the ascendancy of scientistic ideology in literary studies. It was the same evolution as in the literary world itself, with naturalism giving way to symbolism and its sequels, but in the universities it occurred later because of the institutional entrenchment of the positivistic ideology. The organization of academic studies, and the small number of chairs, turned universities into well-defended fortresses against the forces of change.

And yet, in the end, the myth of literary history as a science of literature failed. One reason, of course, was the ambiguous nature of the beast. One cannot talk about literature without becoming at least minimally involved with literary interpretation in the wider sense. One cannot discuss a novel or a play without touching upon the "psychology" of the characters. One cannot present Balzac or Dickens and say nothing of their views of modern society or of the relationships between rich and poor in nineteenth-century Europe. One cannot be a literary historian, in other words, without being a little bit of everything. And this is what a good literary historian really is— an interdisciplinary scholar *avant la lettre*.

The notion of literary history as a well-circumscribed field is an illusion that did not have to be denounced to affect its practitioners negatively and undermine their rather naïve conception of literary studies.

At the time when literary history triumphed, the social sciences were in a dynamic and expansive mood. They, too, were "positivistic" in the old sense and genuinely convinced that they could elaborate truly scientific ways of accounting for man and his various activities.

Even if they wanted to, literary people would have been unable to criticize this illusion, and most literary historians did not want to. They shared the scientistic optimism of their colleagues in the social sciences.

As a result, they felt more and more amateurish and impressionistic. They did not possess the formal training needed to turn them into the professional psychologists, sociologists, and anthropologists that they should have been to speak competently about the various themes of many literary works.

Thus students of literature were increasingly ill at ease when discussing the content of literary works. They began to wonder whether their discipline could do more than provide useful but peripheral information about literature, supplemented with some amiable chatter about its content.

If professional psychologists alone are competent to deal with the psychological aspects of literature, professional sociologists with the sociological aspects, anthropologists with the mythical or ritual aspects, and so on, the specialist of literature is left empty-handed.

Everything that had anything to do with the *content* of literature came to be regarded with suspicion by literary people, who felt uncomfortable with it—and even with the dreams of a writer, since there was a Sigmund Freud by that time to claim that he had turned our dreams into a genuine science.

The scientific aspirations of literary studies were undermined not only by the growing influence of the neo-romantics but by the field's own conceptual weakness, by its inability to define an object that would be unambiguously its own.

As a result, there was a good deal of pressure, from the early twentieth century on, for literary studies to discover its own specificity. To be protected against the encroachment of imperialistic disciplines that were not literary, literary studies needed to define some pure essence of literature, something that would justify its existence as an autonomous academic enterprise.

This pressure was intense in Russia after the revolution, when one could still hope to protect intellectual life from simplistic Marxism through intellectual means, and this resulted in Russian formalism.

Pressure was felt in America, too, especially after World War II, when the prestige of science was at its peak and departmental organization generated a competition for funds between the social sciences and the humanities.

The most precious aspect of literature, the one most worthy of being studied, had to be whatever is left of a work of art when it has been emptied of its content. At this point, it was natural for literary studies to rediscover the old opposition of form and content, which seemed the perfect vehicle for hard-pressed literary critics in their effort to find something in the literary work that no one could steal from them.

The avant-garde of the time proclaimed that the real purpose of literary studies was the examination of form. Content was declared more or less irrelevant and rather lowly stuff anyway, dreadfully unpoetical and materialistic, and worthy only of the social scientists who made it their business to soil their hands with it.

The beauty of a work was in its form exclusively. Form was exalted in terms reminiscent of the plastic arts or of shipbuilding. The great drawback, except in the case of poems that exhibited the same formalistic and idealistic bias held by critics themselves, was that this celebration of form was not conducive to concrete emphasis on the work itself, which was supposed to be the goal of the whole enterprise.

Formalistic studies were becoming more and more unsubstantial. This background is necessary to understand why the new European methodologies of structuralism and deconstruction as represented by such figures as Barthes, Lévi-Strauss, Foucault, and Derrida were so successful in this country. The emphasis was on structural linguistics in the Saussurian and Jakobsonian manner. For both Ferdinand de Saussure and Roman Jakobson, language is a system of diacritical signs that signify in opposition to one another, rather than in immediate and unchangeable relationship to the things they signify.

Saussurian linguistics became a means to confirm and reinforce the expulsion of "content." The "signifier" corresponds to "form," the hierarchically inferior "signified" becomes the new word for "content," and the despised "referent" the new word for reality.

More than ever, the humanities were eager to declare their independence from the mundane university, which was busy with the "real world." At the same time, structural linguistics was privileged because one part of it, phonemics, was built on a finite set of variables, unlike the older social sciences, which used ordinary language. Was it legitimate for the literary "applications" of structuralism to claim a scientific status on this basis? No one believes this anymore, but for a time many people did.

Structuralism seemed able to reconcile the scientific impulse, on the one hand, and the romantic feeling of a literary transcendence, on the other. This was a very powerful and potent combination, which explains the fascination that structuralism and even post-structuralism have exerted on literary studies.

Structuralism was developed in the context of the social sciences, but it was successful primarily in literary and philosophical circles. This movement has enabled literary circles to conduct a kind of counterattack against the imperialism of the social sciences. The precise form of this counterattack came from the fact that the social sciences use ordinary language in a noncritical way. At the beginning of the twentieth century, a French writer named Paul Valéry was already suggesting that the social sciences are little more than mediocre literature, meaning fiction. They are a form of literature unaware that it consists of language. The good thing about creative writers is their awareness of language. They know that language is treacherous, and they deliberately use rhetorical means to achieve certain effects. Social scientists are doing the same thing but with no real awareness of it—a dreadful *esprit de sérieux*. They have a naïve faith in facts, as if they could reach the facts directly, whereas in reality they reach only their own words. They mistake words for things, and this is the real meaning of the title of Michel Foucault's *Les Mots et les choses*.[1]

The movement was launched in earnest by Claude Lévi-Strauss, who was the first social scientist to criticize the social sciences of his time from the point of view of their language. But Lévi-Strauss immediately turned around and tried to establish structural linguistics as the model for a new type of social science, structural anthropology. In my opinion, this attempt has completely failed. Post-structuralism continued to rely on structural linguistics to discredit the referentiality of all texts.

In his most characteristic works, Jacques Derrida joins Lévi-Strauss and Foucault in insisting that we can and must undermine all philosophical systems, all philosophical texts, with the help of structural linguistics. But he goes on to argue that the reverse is also true: we must undermine any scheme that would base itself on structural linguistics, with the help of philosophical language and philosophical texts. The truth is that there is no truth in any text, except perhaps for the truth of an absence of truth, and even that is not quite certain. Even the most prudently acrobatic and Derridian uses of language remain prisoners of the fundamental conceptual illusion of Western metaphysics—namely, our instinctive trust in the

[1] Michel Foucault, *The Order of Things* (New York, 1970).

substantiality and stability of language. This instinctive trust in language is characteristic of a younger culture whose faith in reality is inseparable from its faith in itself. In contrast, deconstruction and its attitudes are the product of an aging and terribly disenchanted culture. Deconstruction tries to show that, if handled correctly, any system of thought will ultimately self-destruct.

True or false, this bleak nihilism appeals to people who feel that they are at the bottom of the ladder, on the last rung, and that if the ladder itself collapses everybody on it will fall down; they have nothing to lose. But literature will come out on top because, at its best, it does not take itself seriously. Literature is aware that it turns language into play, instead of being the involuntary plaything of a language in which it believes. Deconstruction is a weapon turned against the idea of truth.

Deconstruction originates in a spirit of mimetic rivalry with the social sciences. This spirit always turns the rivals into identical twins, and this paradoxical effect can be observed in our present situation. Even though the social sciences and deconstruction are poles apart philosophically, their ultimate impact on intellectual life and on the academic world is strikingly similar. This, I think, is one of the most curious consequences of the present situation.

Blind faith in deconstructive methodologies and the extreme seriousness with which they are taken in the United States have resulted in the neglect of our great cultural tradition in favor of the latest research. Too much respect for the latest research is dangerous, because statistically there are not that many geniuses at any given moment in the history of any culture, and a bit of sifting is needed to separate the wheat from the chaff. The social sciences believe, or pretend to believe, that the latest research is necessarily superior to what came before simply because it comes later. So do the media. They all believe that knowledge is progressive and cumulative. This belief is extremely convenient. Even if we are not very good ourselves, we enjoy all the benefits of past research, plus the benefits of our own. We may be dwarfs, but we stand on the shoulders of giants, and ultimately we are greater than these giants. This is a dangerously complacent illusion. If such things as experience, personal insight, talent, and hard knocks are important in our ability to acquire any kind of knowledge, especially in human affairs, this belief in progress is disastrous for the transmission of the highest culture. It never considers the possibility that the most recent research might turn out to be no more than the ephemeral product of fad and fashion—cultural garbage that, fifty years later, no one will read. Yet experience shows us that this has already happened to a large extent, and it is probable that it will happen again in the future.

Radical theory and deconstructive theory do not believe in cumulative knowledge. They criticize this myth, sometimes too harshly, because in certain areas there really is such a thing as cumulative knowledge. According to a strange paradox, however, they end up behaving in exactly the same way as the social sciences. Knowledge is not cumulative, but deconstruction and its projected disintegration of Western illusions are, at least up to a point. Deconstruction is a long and arduous task that demands the allegiance of many workers. Deconstructionists do not believe in progress in the old sense, but they believe in progress in the battle against Western metaphysics, and their concrete position is a mirror image of the belief in progress. Every ten years or so, we have a new batch of deconstructive literature that claims to render the previous batch outmoded. The latest research is supposed to be so much more radical and so much more revolutionary than the previous research that it is completely unnecessary to read the old fogies. If one wanted to be really polemical, one could say that faith in the progress of knowledge has been replaced by faith in the progress of ignorance. Let us hope that this second faith will prove to be as unfounded as the first one was.

Deconstruction is to the false knowledge it deconstructs a little like the antimatter of the physicist in its relationship to matter: they behave in exactly the same way, so that it is difficult to distinguish one from the other. A century ago, the belief in cumulative and progressive knowledge destroyed the role that Greek and Latin culture had long played in our education. Today, the belief in an anti-progress is destroying the role that modern and classical literature played in our education only a few years ago. This, however, may be too pessimistic a view. I exaggerate to make my point clear. It must be observed, in all fairness, that the original leaders of the movement try to react against the anti-intellectual consequences of some of

their doctrines. They insist that, even though philosophical discourse possesses an inherently illogical
foundation, it must be studied because it is the
strongest discourse available and cannot be dispensed
with.

With many epigones, however, no such precautions
are taken. I recall, for instance, an incident a few years
ago at a great East Coast university that had become
a kind of revolving door for the fiercest theorists of all
stripes. When I was teaching there, the students were
in a state of almost catatonic apathy, which was
briefly interrupted by fits of frenzied activity. They
felt that they were under permanent attack, that there
were plots against deconstruction as a whole, and that
both the rest of the university and many deconstructionists as well were their enemies. They were divided into slightly different versions of the same ideology, completely indistinguishable from one another
to the uninitiated, but to them as different as night
and day. They felt that the fate of the world depended
on the redemptive value of the particular brand of nihilism they were promoting in literary studies.

One day, one of the students, a charming young
woman, was going through some rhapsody of her own
composition; we were all swimming laboriously in a
murky ocean of Anglo-Franco-Teutonic jargon when
suddenly I caught her saying something about a
prophet of the school that was absolutely false—I
knew it for a fact because I had been a witness of the
event. I did not want to waste my one and only chance
to say something relevant to her talk, and I interrupted her with alacrity. After listening to what I had

to say, she put on a gentle but slightly condescending smile and said, "But you don't understand. You are too old. We are already third generation deconstructionists, and we read only the second generation. We don't have to read Derrida himself, who has been deconstructed quite a few years ago. We can completely dispense with that sort of thing." It is nice to see that American optimism will reassert itself even in the most desperate circumstances, but the cultural results can be a little weird, to say the least.

Deconstructionism is not, of course, entirely responsible for the situation we have today. The mechanics of an academic career in the United States has a lot to do with the worst features of "criticism" today. There are very good aspects to literary studies in this country, but there are also aspects that are not so good, and they should be debated openly, for if we remain silent we will go from bad to worse.

Assistant professors at American universities are extremely interested in a strange institution called academic tenure. The path to tenure is publication, and in all my years of teaching, the law of "publish or perish" is the only one that has survived every cultural revolution. To publish, you must have something to write about. This "something" is supposed to be at least slightly different from what other people have already published. It is difficult to say something genuinely new and original. It is relatively easy, however, to simulate originality by saying the opposite of what your immediate predecessors have said, especially if they are the only people you have read and studied.

The danger today is that people who do genuinely brilliant work will be overshadowed by the ebb and flow of fads and fashions that have little substance and that are hardly more than a collective form of *esprit de contradiction*: the shift from one abstract extreme to another. This is not only true of literary criticism. If we look at all fields, ranging from sociology to ethology to dietetics, we find hordes of hungry researchers trying to overturn the theories of their predecessors every ten years. They embrace these theories in reverse form to gain tenure at little intellectual cost. The top becomes the bottom and the bottom becomes the top. Ten years ago, for instance, when ethology was very much in fashion, we heard that animals are much sweeter creatures than man and that they never resort to murder. This was the optimistic spirit of 1968. In 1988, animals do commit murder after all.

Every day, new examples appear that contradict the literature of ten years ago. In the strange world of contemporary studies, it is often hard to distinguish how much of the strangeness results from the creative genius of so-called radical theory, and how much from the social and organizational conditions of academic life today.

Let us consider two major principles of deconstructive criticism in the light of requirements for tenure. The deconstructionists have been saying, quite eloquently and at great length, that interpretation is infinite. There is no limit to the number of interpretations that can legitimately be made of the same texts, even of non-literary texts, whatever that means. The same is true of the interpretations one could give of these first interpretations. Each time I reread a text, whether I like it or not, I produce an interpretation that is different from my previous interpretations. Each one of these can and should be published. This is good news indeed in an academic system that demands that each assistant professor publish at least one book-length essay in his field of specialization as a requirement for tenure, regardless of how inflated the literature in that field already is. The good news is that it is impossibile to interpret any text to death.

We live in a world where plagiarism has become a philosophical impossibility. It simply cannot exist. If a dean tells you that there can be such a thing, she must belong to some benighted field like computer science. This is very good news indeed. It is so good that literary critics should be discreet about it for fear of appearing a little self-serving.

A few years ago, I remember listening to a great pontiff of deconstruction from the East Coast. Speaking as an academic critic, he loudly congratulated himself as he beheld an eternal future in which the entire world would be regarded as a text interpreting itself—everybody interpreting everybody else—until the end of the world. When you consider that any respectable English department in this country must have at least one Milton specialist, it is wonderful to know that Saudi Arabian oil will run out before we exhaust possible interpretations of *Paradise Lost*. Before the advent of radical theory, Milton specialists could not help but feel vaguely uncomfortable with the thought that, perhaps after the ten-thousandth book on Milton, the most respected scholars would decide to declare a moratorium on all future Milton publications. Thanks to recent advances in critical theory, even that remote danger has been eliminated once and for all. We can look forward to a brave new world in which even ten million books on Milton will not begin to make a dent in the material available for interpretation.

A second principle of deconstructive criticism, which flows from the first, is that no interpretation can be said to be better or worse than any other. All are equally good. I even heard someone say once at a symposium that all interpretations are equally *indispensable*. When you remember that our interpretations are absolutely infinite in number, the idea that they are all indispensable becomes as scary as science fiction stories in which mutants invade the whole planet.

In this new context, the idea that certain publications might not be good enough to be counted toward tenure no longer makes any philosophical sense. The belief that writing can be good or bad is a "metaphysical" prejudice to which academic deans tend to cling because they usually come from the sciences and from the stodgiest fields of the humanities; they cannot understand or appreciate the brave new world that the avant-garde is bringing about.

These are, I realize, cheap shots, and I apologize for my self-indulgence. If there is any relevance to what I say, it does not pertain to the best of deconstruction, but to something called the sociology of literature, a concrete sociology of literature that takes the university into account as a social institution. Many critics over the last fifty years have tried to reduce great works of art to the social circumstances of their creation. In my view, they have not been successful. I am not a Marxist, and I am not suggesting that this type of reductionism should be practiced. But it does seem that, if there is a historical period that is particularly amenable to Marxist criticism, it must be our own. Within our period, I would say, there is one literary genre that is particularly amenable to Marxist criticism: literary criticism itself.

Because of tenure requirements, literary criticism has become a kind of minor industry. It is also the only economic activity that escapes the kind of fiercely suspicious criticism to which all other literary genres are now subjected by this same criticism. Hence I would suggest that all radical theories, including Marxist theory, turn their attention on themselves and concentrate on their own mechanisms of production. These mechanisms, in my view, verify the principles of Marxist theory more strikingly than any phenomenon of the past. Our critical theories are wonderfully true because they are self-fulfilling prophecies. If the world about which they speak did not exist at the moment these theories were elaborated, we need not worry. Give them a little time and their very popularity will generate the world whose existence they postulate. The world in which Western humanistic and ethical values have become meaningless is really upon us, and, of course, it is the world of deconstructive theory.

Thus deconstruction tends to function in exactly

the same way as the social sciences it attempts to rival. Today, in fact, this counterattack is remarkably successful. The area where deconstructive criticism is truly on the march is no longer literature, where it has probably reached its zenith, but in departments of history and other social sciences, which no doubt have good reasons to feel a little dubious about themselves and their own methods. Deconstructive criticism could not have the influence it does on these disciplines if it were not for its tendency to divorce itself from our cultural tradition in a manner quite reminiscent of the social sciences themselves. Deconstruction may yet bring back to the social sciences that self-confidence and intolerance they once had, which seem to be on the decline at the present time.

Despite what I have said, I do not really believe that deconstruction and the other radical theories are the principal cause of our crisis. They are more a symptom than a cause. There are other causes, and some of them are so vast that they cannot be considered in the framework of a brief essay. I do think, however, that others are specific to the academic world, and that we should examine them just as critically as we examine the social context of nonacademic phenomena. The increase in the academic population over the last thirty years, the broadening of the base of higher education, plus the great wealth of American universities, where teachers have ten or fifteen students, have led to an enormous multiplication of the number of professors. This has transformed our world into one so different from the nineteenth- and even from the early twentieth-century university that the use of the same word to designate the two is probably misleading.

If you consider our numbers in the abstract, you might think we are about the right size for a harmonious and productive intellectual life. How many of us are there in the humanities? How many members does the Modern Language Association have? There must be at least twenty thousand active people. We complain about the indifference of the outside world. The public pays no attention to us; it is not interested in criticism; yet our numbers correspond, more or less, to the actual audiences of Shakespeare or Racine at the time they were writing. Our sector of the academic world is as large as the entire cultivated public of Elizabethan England or the France of Louis the Fourteenth.

And yet our cultural world is a far cry from Elizabethan England or *la cour et la ville* in seventeenth-century France. There is a reason for this, so simple and so obvious that no one ever mentions it. At the time of Elizabeth and Louis, one percent, perhaps, of the educated people were producers, and ninety-nine percent were consumers. The ninety-nine percent were truly interested in what was produced. With us, the proportion is curiously reversed. We are supposed to live in a world of consumerism, but in the university there are only producers. We are under a strict obligation to write, and therefore we hardly have the time to read one another's work. It is very nice, when you give a lecture, to encounter someone who is not publishing, because perhaps that person has not only enough curiosity but enough time to read your books.

I myself feel guilty because I do not spend enough time reading my contemporaries. In many universities today it has been decided that, to be promoted to associate professor with tenure, you must write two books. I hear that, in some instances, the tenure guidelines specify that these books be important enough to "revolutionize" the field. If an assistant professor must revolutionize his field twice before he can get tenure, he can read absolutely nothing outside that field. He has to cheat all along the line. He is totally unable to keep up with neighboring disciplines.

These requirements are absurd. The situation is a disaster. The demands of an academic career are incompatible with the requirements of a meaningful intellectual life, and this fact should be faced openly. No wonder such phenomena as mass guruism and the fanatical embrace of pseudo-radicalism occur. Many people don't even read the gurus' books, but they do exchange gossip about these teachers and make jokes about their sexual escapades as though they were movie stars or famous athletes. The same people who do this also create subsections of a subsection of a subsection at MLA meetings, devoted to an analysis of, for instance, feminism in northern Albania between 1922 and 1923. Their real desire is to reconstruct the community that they are deprived of, which the university can no longer provide.

The tendency of graduate students today to apply for admission to comparative literature or to so-called interdisciplinary programs, and their fascination with all theories that still talk about the global picture, even if negatively, is basically a healthy one. It stems from a need to re-create an intellectual life that is real. The situation is especially discouraging to the best people because, even though there is a romantic myth that we all write for our own pleasure and do not need readers, the truth of the matter is quite different. If you really have ideas, you want them to be tested against the ideas of other people. The present system is creating vast reservoirs of resentment—reservoirs of legitimate resentment, because those who have ideas receive no echoes from their colleagues.

We live in a world where the very ease of communication has become the greatest barrier to meaningful communication. Instead of improving the situation, knowledge retrieval schemes and computerized monstrosities can only make it worse.

The truth is that only the individual human being can give us the recognition we all seek, and the capacity of this individual mind to read and assimilate books is finite. If you create a world in which production is as excessive as it is today, everything in it tends to appear equally insignificant from an intellectual point of view. Even the best material is likely to go unnoticed and remain forever unread. The very size and organization of our intellectual life creates a reserve army for our current and future nihilistic enterprises. I would be surprised if the future did not have fads and fashions in store for us that will make the present ones look quite tame in comparison. Ours still have a few redeeming features, if you make allowances for the context in which they have appeared. The truth is that a certain complacent humanism has collapsed—the humanism of the "great books" courses—which is associated with a belief in the automatic carryover of technical advances into the intellectual field.

My view, however, is that the great texts of our literature are intact. They are totally unaffected by what has happened during the last fifty years. Earlier, I suggested that the radical methodologies of the present are rebellious children of a New Criticism and of a formalism that has emptied literature of its content. We have to go back to that content.

To give an example of what I mean, I will first go back to *esprit de contradiction*. Why and when does contradiction become an *esprit*? When it spreads like the plague to dominate and distort every argument. The life of the mind needs contradiction as a stimulus, but too much of it kills genuine creativity.

Intellectual movements can die of not enough contradiction, and they can also die of an overdose, especially in France. The fatal disease begins deceptively enough. It produces an excitement that seems to be the height of "creativity" and "innovation." Like a malignant fever, it flushes the cheeks of those it is about to devour.

Many instances of this process have been recorded but, significantly, by playwrights and novelists rather than philosophers, in works that philosophy would never regard as valid descriptions of its own processes.

Molière's Alceste is marvelously French but also non-French, a valid portrait of the modern intellectual that remains pertinent to this day. Molière did immortalize our type in highly favorable circumstances: a certain mode of intellectual life was beginning to disintegrate—call it "French classicism," the "salon," or whatever. Negative thinking was on the march, and Alceste was leading that march.

To understand the man, you must go beyond his arguments in favor of ecology and old-fashioned virtue. This first Alceste is for the birds, or rather for Philinte and Rousseau, who were made for each other, as well as for the *petits marquis* and the traditional critics. The real Alceste, the profound Alceste, is the one portrayed by Célimène. She alone is his equal and she alone understands him. If you are as gifted as Alceste and Célimène are, in a university as well as in a salon, success will make you a coquette, and failure a misanthrope. Is it purely a question of language? Almost but not quite, like everything in human affairs.

Classical genius reduced Alceste to a single but supremely relevant feature—*esprit de contradiction*, the inevitable correlative of his famous "Je veux qu'on me distingue" and the sign of his power, and impotence, in a world exclusively dedicated to language, like our own, and just as competitive.

> Et ne faut-il pas bien que Monsieur contredise?
> A la commune voix veut-on qu'il se réduise,
> Et qu'il ne fasse pas éclater en tous lieux
> L'esprit contrariant qu'il a reçu des cieux?
> Le sentiment d'autrui n'est jamais pour plaire;
> Il prend toujours en main l'opinion contraire,
> Et penserait paraître un homme du commun,

Si l'on voyait qu'il fut de l'avis de quelqu'un.
L'honneur de contredire a pour lui tant de charmes,
Qu'il prend contre lui-même assez souvent des armes;
Et ses vrais sentiments sont combattus par lui,
Aussitôt qu'il les voit dans la bouche d'autrui.

(Molière, *Le Misanthrope*, II, iv, 669–80)

(And is not this gentleman bound to contradict? Would you have him subscribe to the general opinion; and must he not everywhere display the spirit of contradiction with which Heaven has endowed him? Other people's thoughts can never please him. He always supports a contrary idea, and he would think himself too much of the common herd, were he observed to be of anyone's opinion but his own. The honour of gainsaying has so many charms for him, that he very often takes up the cudgels against himself; he combats his own sentiments as soon as he hears them from other people's lips.)

This portrait is really the key to everything Alceste says and does, from his ridiculous controversy with Oronte to his unforgivable behavior when he tries to court Eliante just to spite Célimène. *Esprit de contradiction* is a more elegant, powerful, and even courteous interpretation of his conduct than the *hypocrisy* with which he perpetually clubs everybody over the head, even though he is the one who most deserves to be clubbed.

The difference between a university and a salon is that you cannot have a salon unless you remain on speaking terms with the people in it. Even though Alceste prefigures our own bad manners in his fits of silent pouting, he occasionally comes out of them to vituperate Célimène and her flatterers. Not so with us. We speak only to our own schools of thought.

Our intellectual machines have become so efficient that, at the very instant a potential opponent begins to speak, he disqualifies himself. By opening his un-initiated mouth, he reveals that he still partakes of that grossly naïve and ancestral confidence in language of which twentieth-century philosophies liberate their devotees.

Long before the military, we have invented the Star Wars of intellectual life. We can shoot down enemy missiles at the very instant they leave their silos. The only problem, of course, is that we bring intellectual life to a standstill.

One can distinguish two main phases in postwar French intellectual life, characterized by an increasingly virulent and self-destructive *esprit de contradiction*.

The first phase was Hegelian and relatively optimistic. Countless errors had to be crushed through generous applications of stern demystification, but beyond the carnage a faint hope glimmered. Like the happy ending of old movies, universal *synthesis* was always around the corner.

Orthodox Sartrism belongs to this phase, but it also represents a strategic retreat into the self. Negative thinking concentrates its poisons to use them more efficiently against all comers. Sartre's faith in the possibility of *having a philosophy* looks startlingly naïve, however, from the deconstructive point of view.

At its paroxysm, *esprit de contradiction* turns

against itself and destroys its own crystal palaces in order to forestall their possible destruction by others. It denounces philosophy as a huge contradiction of which it is a part, even though it is also heroically fighting a patient battle against the universal illusion.

This is the deconstructive phase, when the negative spirit becomes so clever that it disappears as such. It can always stay a step ahead of everyone, so it becomes impregnable. Molière captured the dynamics of this escalation; Célimène's last lines are dedicated to self-contradiction.

Célimène herself is an even better example than Alceste. She is the arch-deconstructionist. She contradicts herself as much as he does, but she no longer tries to hide it. She turns it into a novel kind of superiority. When convenient, she does not hesitate to discard the ancient ideal of self-consistency.

The assault on truth always comes at the end of a competitive escalation about truth. All such escalations divide into two main phases. The first is a positive phase in which everyone tries to reach a certain type of "truth." It ends in a deadlock, with everyone advocating his own "truth" against all the other "truths." At some point, everyone gives up the search simultaneously, mimetically, and the rivalry shifts to the demonstration of how impossible it is to reach any kind of truth.

Formalism already belonged to that phase, but discreetly, through its minimization of *content*. Structuralism is the same, with a vengeance—it is a more radical way to evacuate "content," and post-structuralism is an even more radical one. To exalt the signified at the expense of the referent, and the signifier at the expense of the signified, is always to dismantle the still positive something that had survived until then. Structuralism is an excellent analysis of what happens to culture when *esprit de contradiction* takes over.

Our only mistake is to believe that this process is everything, that there is nothing beyond it. Oppositions are not all that matter. Structuralism is *esprit de contradiction* shooting itself in the foot. Poststructuralism is that wounded foot grabbing the pistol and shooting back at the entire body.

In one essential respect, our deconstructive stage of German idealism resembles language analysis in its heyday. The two schools belong to the negative phase of two philosophical escalations that take language and truth as their objects and end up regarding both as annihilated once and for all by their own negative process, the force of which they grossly exaggerate, just as Célimène, intelligent though she is, exaggerates the importance of her salon. How awesome is the power of critical thinking once you no longer believe in words—except, of course, if they happen to be your own!

Molière could not imagine our world, but he shows us one in which the comic and tragic outline of our own is retroactively visible. Only the playwright or novelist treats the comedy of the intellect as the human interaction that it always is, even and especially when it refuses to recognize itself as such.

To me, the content of the *Misanthrope*, or its referent, or what you will, is Célimène on *esprit de con-tradiction*. Whichever way you call it, this is the sort of thing our literary criticism has systematically neglected, and it begs to be studied. This content is about ourselves *together*—not about society as a whole, and not about myself as an individual, a solitary *Dasein*, a Freudian unconscious, or anything else.

This *content* is specific to Western dramas and novels at their best. Our real motivation for eluding it is not that the psychoanalysts or the sociologists are more competent to deal with it than we are. The competence of literary critics is a negative one. They do not have to pay allegiance to some pseudo-science. They have the greatest texts. If literary critics, too, keep eluding the content of these texts, they must have some other reason, which may well be truth itself. Especially in human affairs, nothing is as unpopular as truth.

If we look at deconstruction as the child of New Criticism, we will understand that it entered a literary world from which content had already been expelled. I think we must return to content. We must not be intimidated by linguistic terrorism. Linguistic terrorism makes all reference impossible to reach. My own work has convinced me that the most perspicacious texts from the standpoint of human relations are the great texts of Western literature. They do not have to be studied from a Marxist or a Freudian point of view to yield what they have to yield; indeed, they must counterattack. We must counter with literature as a whole, instead of attacking the social sci-

ences with an impoverished notion of what literature
is.

Radical theory tells us today that the notion of the
masterpiece is completely outdated, and that the so-
called best works were chosen arbitrarily or as a way
of manipulating power. I do not believe this at all. Go
to writings that have not been sanctioned by poster-
ity and you will quickly discover that in literature we
have a tremendous advantage. We have the greatest
texts in the world. When a social scientist writes a
great book, which does happen from time to time, it
must be discarded ten years later because new research takes its place. What happens to that text?
Sooner or later the literary people inherit it. Literature is the repository of all great texts that exist outside of fashion. Therefore we must not become the
victims of fashion. I believe that the canon of great
texts is meaningful. I feel we can rejuvenate our studies from the inside. When we reconquer the content
of our literary works, we will reconquer the ground
lost to the social sciences without resorting to the ter-
rorist methods of what the French call *la politique du
pire*: the policy of choosing the worst option to destroy your enemy, even though you are destroyed at
the same time. That is terrorism. We have no right to
feel demoralized, discouraged, resentful, and under-
privileged. We are sitting on a great treasure whose
value far too many of us underestimate. If we learn to
make that treasure fructify, the future belongs to us.